# ONE SIMPLE THING

*Simple Tools for Living
Your Own
Theory of Change*

In praise of

# ONE SIMPLE THING

*Simple Tools for Living*
*Your Own Theory of Change*


"The heart of this book is Change. Through a realistic and engaging reader-centered process, Dr. Tytel offers the reader a valuable set of Simple Tools and an uncomplicated approach to transformation. **One Simple Thing** asks highly important questions, allows time for reflection, and provides crisp, clear examples to support you in pursuing your own best self. "

        Janet Holston
        Director of Special Initiatives
        Arizona State University


"Mallary is an absolute inspiration! By offering **One Simple Thing** and this collection of Simple Tools, she thoughtfully guides us through an enlightening process to best understand the core, "sweet spot" of self. While the process is quite rigorous, Mallary presents the concepts and approach in a safe, step-by-step manner which enables the reader to achieve the highest level of success. The results are positively transformational."

        Diane Tiger
        Dean, Vanguard University
        The Vanguard Group

"Focusing on One Simple Thing truly makes a world of difference. I was introduced to Mallary and her work while struggling to find balance and an open path forward. With her help I devised a solid plan of action, personally and professionally, focusing on concrete change. **One Simple Thing** can indeed make a huge difference."

        Stephen Gittins
        Photographer
        Capture 12 Gallery


"Change is always difficult and so I look for simple solutions. If you change one thing it shifts everything else – and simple can really be transformative in the best way! **One Simple Thing** is a great resource for guiding you through your own process and finding your own path."

        Dr. Christi Olson
        Stanford University
        National Accelerator Laboratory


"This is a wonderful exploration of our own inherent ability to create change and profoundly impact the world. With **One Simple Thing**, the author offers an inspiring demonstration of the application and appeal of one's own Theory of Change, and how the smallest changes can truly make a difference. This is a book for everyone."

        Timothy Germany
        Retired Commissioner
        Federal Mediation and Conciliation Service

## Also by Mallary Tytel

Vision Driven:
Lessons Learned from the Small Business
C-Suite

## Co-authored with Royce Holladay

Simple Rules:
A Radical Inquiry into Self

Radical Inquiry Journal:
A Companion to Simple Rules

# ONE SIMPLE THING

*Simple Tools for Living
Your Own
Theory of Change*

**MALLARY TYTEL**

To contact the author with comments or to inquire about speaking, coaching or consulting opportunities: mallary@simplerulesfoundation.org.

Please be sure to visit the Simple Rules Foundation at www.simplerulesfoundation.org

---

One Simple Thing
Simple Tools for Living your Own Theory of Change

All Rights Reserved.
Copyright © 2015 by Mallary Tytel

Cover Artwork courtesy of Briar Press.

This book may not be reproduced, transmitted, or stored in whole or in part by any means, including graphic, electronic, or mechanical without the express written consent of the publisher except in the case of brief quotations embodied in critical articles and reviews.

Gold Canyon Press
P.O. Box 2223
Apache Junction, Arizona  85217-2223 U.S.A.

www.goldcanyonpress.com
www.simplerulesfoundation.org

PB ISBN:  978-0-9821112-7-7
PRINTED IN THE UNITED STATES OF AMERICA

**This is for Jess and Brad**

*The creation of a thousand forests is in one acorn.*
—Ralph Waldo Emerson

**IF** I can access a set of simple tools to see and understand my actions and how they are helping or harming me, understand who I am, what is important, and how I want to connect with others in the world, and create a basic framework to guide my patterns of thought, behavior, and decision-making,

**THEN** I can identify and accomplish One Simple Thing every day to reach my goal and realize a productive, sustainable, and fit life.

# Acknowledgments

It is with great appreciation and affection that I recognize and express my thanks to those incredible individuals who provided their time, energy, wisdom, and support to making this book a reality.

Thanks to Glenda Eoyang, executive director and founder of the Human Systems Dynamics Institute. Glenda changes the world every day. As a teacher, mentor, and friend she has helped sow the seeds from which my learning and practice have continued to grow.

Thanks to my colleague and friend Royce Holladay for her sense of clarity, insight, and the passion that she brings to this work every day.

Thanks to Patricia Seppanen for the depth and breadth of her knowledge and proficiency in evaluation methodology, her willingness to share, and her sharp wit.

Thanks to the amazing Kathy Shields, Janet Holston, and Laura Orsini for their deft and finely-tuned editorial expertise, consideration, and patience.

And thanks to Melanie Ohm, for her heartfelt gifts of collaboration, celebration, and song.

# Table of Contents

| | |
|---|---|
| Forward | 1 |
| Introduction | 3 |
| Chapter 1. What is One Simple Thing? | 11 |
| Chapter 2. Think Systems | 21 |
| Chapter 3. Patterns | 31 |
| Chapter 4. Radical Inquiry and Simple Rules | 45 |
| Chapter 5. Simple Tools | 61 |
| Chapter 6. Theory of Change | 113 |
| Chapter 7. Simply Acting with Intention | 141 |
| Chapter 8. One Simple Thing for 100 Days | 151 |
| Chapter 9. The Individual, the Whole, and the Greater Whole | 167 |
| References and Resources | 175 |
| About the Author | 181 |

# Forward

I act on the notion that life is an adventure. It thrills us, wounds us, challenges, and celebrates us. It invites us to a deepening awareness of Self and World from vantage points low and high. This past year has been one of extreme adventure for me, demanding an accounting of all of my personal and professional resources. In such a time, when all that is visible is the next step and each decision has extraordinary implications, we must have tools and capacities for change already at hand. Every voyage transforms us. For this, we can thoughtfully prepare.

Mallary recently walked into my life, on the heels of my extraordinary year. She is a sunrise of a soul who sees a new horizon and blazes a path toward it. Here, in her latest book, she designed an exploration of the concept of change. Have you ever felt stuck in a way of living and working that doesn't embody you? Do you have a way of thinking about change that serves your values and ideals? Have you thought about altering the conditions around you to maximize your capacities and realize your potential? Have you ever thought change could hinge on One Simple Thing? Mallary has rolled her experience in human systems dynamics, facilitation, coaching, adaptive action, and change management into a big book with one essential focus at the center – you.

ONE SIMPLE THING

As a gifted writer and storyteller, Mallary simply translates complex ideas into reflective experiences and daily practices that are both intuitive and practical. *One Simple Thing* will provide you with guidance and the tools for change: awareness, creative reflection, communication, and action compelled by a renewed sense of purpose.

If you believe that you are the agent of change for your own life, that you have a responsibility to yourself to be your best self, the path begins here.

Dr. Melanie Ohm
Artist in collaboration and facilitation
Tempe, Arizona USA

# Introduction

*This book is about CHANGE ...*
*and that is why you are here.*

People are about transformation: the movement of energy and matter, behavior and emotion, and the interactions among and between each other. In order to sustain yourself and thrive, you need those things that will advance and nourish you within today's dynamic, unpredictable, and diverse global landscape.

Success, however you define it, requires the critical, skillful use of those principles that produce and maintain the best possible environment for you. These include integrity, values, resources, and optimal conditions for learning, adapting, and growth. Focus should not necessarily be on results but rather on the development and the preservation of structures and practices necessary to deliver the goods.

These "goods" include a range of possibilities and desired outcomes, waiting for you up ahead. Among them are:

- A sense of intention, attainment, performance, and completion while attending to values and the long-term horizon.
- A sense of fairness that centers on how things are done based upon consideration of yourself and others, your community, and connecting with the world.

- A sense of significance as a reminder that what you do, say, and think matters.
- A sense of identity and kinship that bonds you to other people.

When you identify and begin to act in ways that alter the status quo, you may find yourself struggling with standard, long-established methods and models, as well as traditional approaches to measure success. And you likely find that you are stuck.

As my friend Royce often likes to say, "Change is messy." Change drags you out of your comfort zone, for better or for worse, depending upon where you are sitting. Change is also lumbering and awkward – like the first time you lace up a pair of ice skates. You wobble and pitch, without grace or restrain, hurtling across the ice.

That all may be so but you also know this: change is an unavoidable fact of life.

Even when you are looking forward to it in the rosiest of circumstances, change can be thorny. Individuals, communities, and organizations around the world are confronting an increasing range of unknowns. Among these are new and enhanced technology; shifting policies, politics, and values; more turbulent markets; and mounting demands and expectations from family and friends, colleagues and customers, shareholders and stakeholders. All of us are scrambling to meet these predictable and unpredictable challenges, many of which are all about change.

Dr. William Bridges, an expert in the theory and practice of managing human transitions, defines change as moving from one state or condition to another, often though not exclusively due to an external event or situation. For example,

- Your company is relocating across the country, so your own workspace, daily commute, and most likely your job are changing, too.

## Introduction

- After work tomorrow, you are going out for a small celebration with three of your closest friends; you will come home and change into something comfortable and casual for an enjoyable evening.
- Congratulations! You and your spouse are expecting twins! Well, I'd wager that that presents a wellspring of changes ahead.

Accompanying change is "transition," the complete reorientation and reorganization that happens when we are wading through the change process. That includes discovering a brand new neighborhood in your new town; shifting from work mode to play mode at the end of the day; and planning to start two college funds instead of one.

Your feelings about change are often the result of how you manage the path from here to there: What are the challenges? What tools and skills do you have to weather the potential storms? Are you prepared? Your first responses to change may be confusion, questions, doubts, and a feeling of loss. Soon, however, you find yourself moving from denial and resistance to exploration of the possibilities, and finally acceptance and commitment.

While you may not be able to control the change around you, you can decide how you want to navigate through it. For example, think about a recent significant change you came through safely and whole.

- Was it planned or unexpected?
- What was your role throughout the change process?
- What factors were within your control or sphere of influence as your environment shifted?
- How did you feel before, during, and after the transition?
- And right now …?

Now that the turmoil has subsided, you recognize that change is not only inescapable, but change also allows for growth and development. It all depends on you; and managing the process with curiosity, candor, and confidence allows you to build your own strength, capacity, and resilience.

Purposefully initiating change for yourself requires high hopes and solid expectations. Once you make up your mind, begin to hone in on exactly what it is you want to accomplish, and how you are going to accomplish it. Start with these questions:

- What are the conditions or circumstances that need to be present in order to create change?
- Do I understand the "whys" behind my efforts and what I wish to achieve?
- Am I willing to do what it takes to reach and sustain my goals?
- Will I be able to decipher and explain the relationships between and among activities I engage in and their outcomes?
- Do I recognize and appreciate the connections and boundaries that will help me to see, understand, and engage in critical change strategies?

If you are indeed ready to proceed, then it is time to envision a bold, inspiring, possibly unorthodox image in your head of what is possible. Simply let your ideas flow; and whether it is by idle dreaming or conscious intention, this represents a significant shift. You are choosing to become a believer, actor, and doer.

It takes quite a leap of discipline, commitment, and faith for you to move from asking "What is happening here and now?" and "What do I think is going to happen tomorrow?" to "What is my preferred future?" and "What do I need to do to move toward it?"

*Yes, you will craft your own map, One Simple Thing at a time, creating the change you set out to make.*

Introduction

This book offers you a set of Simple Tools to learn about yourself and then create your own Theory of Change – the roadmap to get you from where you are now to where you want to be. And this is a self-directed journey of your own making. You will be able to identify, sustain, and measure your success One Simple Thing at a time, as well as see how every idea, action, connection, and resource align with and support your own values and beliefs.

Watch and discover as one outcome leads to another, and that One Simple Thing can and does make a huge difference.

*There is something very special about seizing the reins and deciding for yourself to embark on significant change. You will hold on to what you know; AND learn new strategies and tactics you have not used before. The time has come: marshal your resources, and take the plunge.*

*Well done!*

## THEORY OF CHANGE

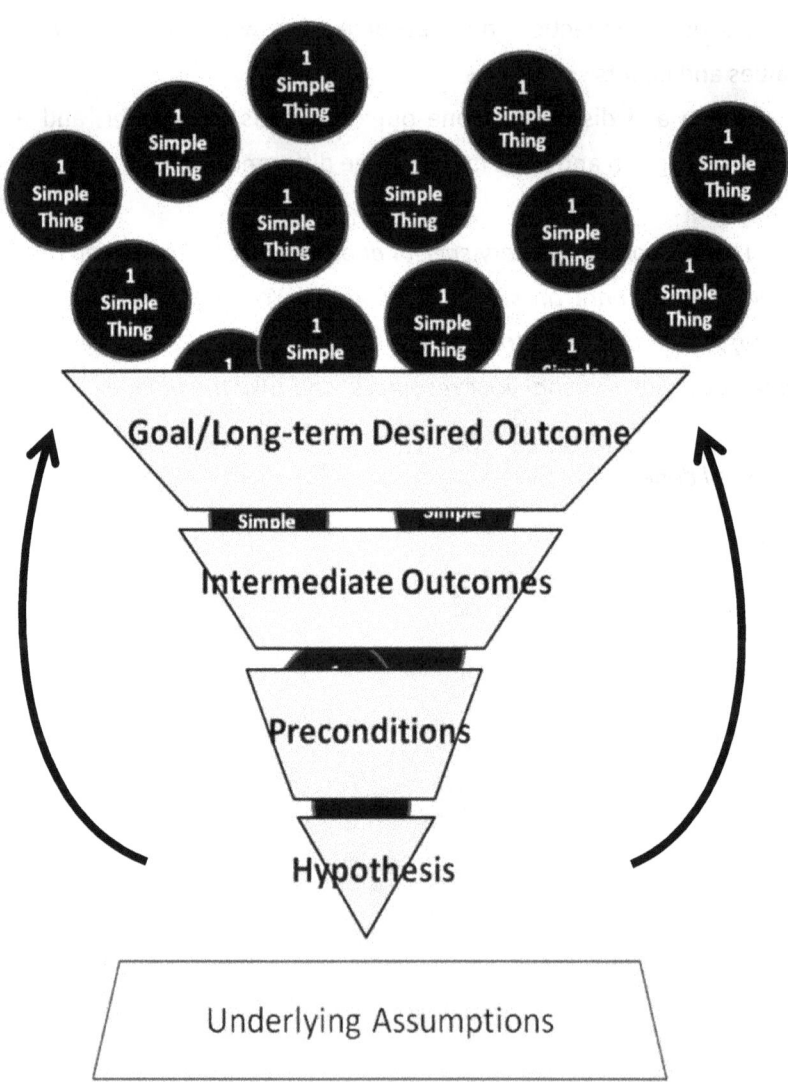

# *ROSA*

In 1900, Montgomery, Alabama, had passed a city ordinance to segregate bus passengers by race. Conductors had the authority to assign seats in support of the ordinance and create white-only and black-only sections. This meant that black riders were required to move when no white-only seats were available.

After a day's work, on December 1, 1955, Rosa Parks, a 42-year-old seamstress boarded the Cleveland Avenue bus. She paid her fare and sat in an empty seat in the first row of the 'colored' section, directly behind the white-only seats. Soon all the white-only seats were filled, and at the next stop several white passengers boarded. The conductor took note, moved the 'colored' section sign behind Parks and demanded that four black people – including Parks – give up their seats. The three other black passengers retreated; not Parks. When threatened with arrest Parks did not back down.

Parks later said, "People always say that I didn't give up my seat because I was tired, but that isn't true. I was not tired physically, or no more tired than I usually was at the end of a working day. No, the only tired I was, was tired of giving in. ... I would have to know for once and for all what rights I had as a citizen and a human being."

The Montgomery Bus Boycott, which was organized for the first day of her trial on December 5, 1955, lasted 381 days.

# Chapter 1. What is One Simple Thing?

*Yes, One Simple Thing can lead to the extraordinary.*

I believe that you have the power to make a difference in your own life and the lives of others. I believe the measure of your humanity has purpose and life from day-to-day. And I believe in the notion of One Simple Thing: that once you are clear about who you are, what is important to you, and how you want to connect with others and the world around you, all you have to do is One Simple Thing every day, and you can change the world. Little things can make a big difference; and you can act in small, purposeful ways to create your own path and be your best self.

Your power lies not in what you can control, but in your ability to influence the world around you. Imagine what might have been if you turned right instead of left last night on your way home and missed the traffic pileup; or you had accepted that first job offer, moved across the state, and never met your significant other; or decided not to stand up at the Town Hall debate and ask that critical follow-up question.

## ONE SIMPLE THING

Each simple action has the potential to alter your life, perhaps even save your life. For example, it is neither hard nor complicated to buckle up your seat belt when you get into your car; and that One Simple Thing actually can save your life. Or think about your favorite alternate-universe fantasy book, film or game, and see the array of *what ifs*. Each of the simple things that George Bailey did or didn't do in the Frank Capra holiday classic *It's a Wonderful Life* changed the lives of his entire community. Or revisit Charles Dickens' *A Christmas Carol,* and notice how the simple things done or left undone transformed Ebenezer Scrooge. What would happen if you whispered a simple word of encouragement in a colleague's ear just when she needed it? If you can see, understand, and act based upon understanding the power of One Simple Thing, you will discover what you are truly capable of.

Now is the time for you to exercise your influence with resolve. Here you are, reading this book, because you want to do something about your world. You want to support resilience, collaboration, and abundance rather than vulnerability, disengagement, and scarcity. You have come to realize that what you are doing doesn't seem to be working anymore and you want to choose another route.

So let's do something different and create change. Begin with the belief that the big questions in life can be disentangled, and your individual strength and actions can crack the code. Each of us can change and better the world by investing in ourselves, each other, and the common good. Let's turn away from fear and hate and deception, and engage others in a better climate: one of reason, respect, and trust.

**Naïve? Perhaps. Easy? No. Simple? Yes!**

The premise of this book is assertive and doable. One simple thought, decision, or action has the power to transform, and this book offers you a set of Simple Tools and a process to create conditions for change. As you

## Chapter 1. What is One Simple Thing?

explore and practice each tool, you will quickly begin to recognize and identify your own patterns of thought and behavior; develop clarity and an understanding of what motivates you; and map out where you are now and where you want to be in the future. Your own fundamental values and beliefs will light your way.

As you experiment with one simple tool after another, new questions will emerge, shining that same light on your next steps. Underlying your learning will be a growing sense of self-awareness and anticipation. And from what you learn about yourself, you will develop your own Theory of Change, identifying the conditions and building the path that will help you reach your goal. Finally, you will start to identify One Simple Thing you can do every day to effect and sustain the change you desire.

This journey will take courage, ingenuity, and stamina: the courage to try, to commit, and to take some risks; the ingenuity to be innovative and resourceful in finding new ways of meeting old, familiar or recurring challenges; and the determination and resilience to keep going, especially when everything and possibly everyone around you seems to say, "Things are not so bad, are they?" That will be for you to decide, and then act with simple purpose.

There is something significant waiting for you up ahead and this is what you will need to carry with you:

- **Attitude.** Do you have the desire and the determination, vision and values, and confidence to get the job done?
- **A tolerance for uncertainty.** Things will not always make sense, and sometimes the answer to the question, "which way?" could be "both" or "neither."
- **Curiosity.** It takes more than finding an answer. It's time to seek out and discover the right questions.

- **Knowing what is important.** Choose wisely, act with intention, and keep your eyes open.
- **Getting to know and understand YOU.** Your own innate abilities will naturally guide your learning and growth.
- **Wanting to make the world a better place for you and others.** Be generous; it is contagious and will multiply before your very eyes.
- **Doing more than what is expected.** Advancement is dependent upon genuine consideration, compassion, caring, and commitment.
- **Being there.** If you are not a member of the team, you cannot be in the game. Your presence is more than just showing up. It is about active participation and contribution.
- **Vision.** Imagine new, healthful, productive, and coherent ways of being engaged in your world. Look around you and envision the potential of all that is possible.

Your achievement will be the ongoing process of striving to go one step further than before, consistently applying a set of simple, clearly-defined actions.

*And just imagine if everybody did that ...*

The notion of One Simple Thing is based on a set of beliefs and hypotheses about the tough yet rewarding work of taking responsibility for yourself and the place you hold in your world. That means creating an environment and a context within which you will thrive.

The experience, expertise, methods, and models shared here have emerged from and are grounded in the theory and practice of many dedicated professionals working in myriad disciplines. They include the fields of human systems dynamics, complexity science, executive coaching, leadership development, culture change, and research and evaluation, among others.

## Chapter 1. What is One Simple Thing?

*Whoa! Right about now you may be thinking: this doesn't sound simple at all. How can One Simple Thing be consistent with complexity, systems, research, evaluation, and other dynamic models? Well, the common denominator here is YOU. Within all of these disciplines, you and everyone else are constantly acting and reacting to what is going on around you; and one simple act can, indeed, change everything. This will become clearer to you as you continue on.*

Consider inhabiting a place that is vital, built on integrity, faith, respect, and fairness, and where differences, inclusion, innovation, and ongoing opportunities for all are fostered. That is a productive and sustainable world.

Now imagine being able to articulate and then achieve your goals, assess and adapt in response to a dynamic, real-world landscape, and maintain an affirming environment of accountability, appreciation, and authenticity. Well, here it is.

This is what is ahead.

- ***Chapter 2 invites you to Think Systems**. This introduction to the nature of systems will help you identify and appreciate how you influence the myriad systems of which you are a part, and how creating change in your own life can lead to change in other parts of your world.

- ***Chapter 3 focuses on Patterns.** Wherever you are, whatever you are engaged in, everything you do creates patterns. Here you will step back and begin to distinguish your own behaviors while (re)discovering your own patterns.

- ***Chapter 4 offers a brief refresher on Radical Inquiry and Simple Rules**, the two models that were the foundation of the book *Simple Rules: A Radical Inquiry into Self* (Holladay and Tytel, Gold Canyon Press, 2011). Understanding and/or revisiting these here will provide an important waypoint on your journey now.

- ***Chapter 5 takes you through the Simple Tools.** These tools build upon each other and help you engage in critical reflection. They provide a "deep dive" into self-awareness, yielding a rich pool of data about YOU. See what surprises or Aha's emerge from your self-exploration.

- ***Chapter 6 introduces you to Theory of Change** and how to build your own change process. As you chart your course to being your best self, you will make the leap from ideas to concrete goals, and then on to action.

- ***Chapter 7 is about Doing: implementing your Theory of Change, doing One Simple Thing every day**, and then assessing your efforts. Examples offered – and your own ideas – will show that simple actions are indeed achievable and yield potent results.

- ***Chapter 8 will help you answer the question, So what do I do now?** Garnered from the work, play, experience, and self-discovery of

## Chapter 1. What is One Simple Thing?

others, you are offered One Simple Thing for 100 Days – one hundred ideas and actions to help stimulate your own thinking and keep you from getting stuck.

- **Chapter 9 helps you integrate your thinking** about yourself, your place in the world, and how each of us contributes to the greater good. It is the "ask" to encourage you to keep moving forward on your own path.

Throughout the book you will also find a series of anecdotes that give strong voice and legs to the assertion that creating productive and sustainable change truly is within your grasp – if you chose to reach for it. These are the stories of real people who implicitly and explicitly have harnessed the power of One Simple Thing. These individual accounts illustrate similarities and differences across a spectrum of circumstances and lives, some of which are familiar, others not.

What you will note is that you need not be sophisticated, brilliant, or in a position of authority to have the power to influence and live your best life. As you read through these individual stories note the building blocks of their own theories of change; and think about chances taken or missed, actual or potential pivotal moments, what might have been, and what you might have done differently.

*Are you willing and able to take advantage of favorable or random circumstances as they present themselves?*

*Can you be ready to act when you find yourself facing unexpected events?*

*Are you prepared to deploy quickly and nimbly at a moment's notice?*

*Can you swiftly recognize an unanticipated yet valuable opportunity or discovery, and then change course, or even history, by making a simple decision or maneuver?*

Read on, choose your path forward, and see what awaits you.

 **Simple Things to Consider:**

*"When all the props and practices of the past no longer work, that is when Change is needed."* —Unknown

## ALEXANDER

Alexander Fleming was a Scottish researcher at St. Mary's Hospital in London. In 1928, he had been experimenting with the influenza virus in his laboratory. Returning from a two-week vacation, he began sorting through his work to pick up where he had left off. He found that many of his cultures, which had been left unattended while he was gone, had to be scrubbed.

He did, however, discover something strange about one particular culture: the dish had become accidently contaminated, and mold had grown all around it. In fact, the mold seemed to have prevented the growth of the staphylococci.

Fleming continued to experiment with the mold, and though he found it killed a large number of bacteria, he simply could not isolate the active element, penicillin. He stopped studying penicillin in 1931 but his research was continued and finished by Howard Flory and Ernst Chain. In 1942, the first patient was successfully treated for streptococcal septicemia in the United States, and penicillin is credited with saving countless lives and limbs of soldiers during World War II.

According to published accounts, Fleming stated: "One sometimes finds what one is not looking for. When I woke up just after dawn on Sept. 28, 1928, I certainly didn't plan to revolutionize all medicine by discovering the world's first antibiotic, or bacteria killer. But I guess that was exactly what I did."

# Chapter 2. Think Systems

Look around and you will see myriad collections of individuals or entities or parts who act in a variety of ways – some of which are predictable, and some of which are unpredictable. These "collections" are **complex adaptive systems** and they include everything from families and communities to ecosystems and weather patterns to school districts and orchestras.

*Complex adaptive systems* are highly diverse, changeable, and contain an infinite number of parts. Some of these parts are individuals, like members of a football team. Their actions are connected, interdependent, and constantly adapting to outside influences, environmental shifts, or other parts of the system. For example, the success of the team's offensive and defensive lines depends upon teammates, the coaching staff, the direction of wind on the field, the opposing players, and even predictions in the media about the outcome of Sunday's game. Each part also has the potential and ability to change and influence everyone and everything around them – all it would take is doing One Simple Thing. A pass interception is not easy, but it is One Simple Thing that can change the course of the game, as well as the immediate disposition of the 60,000 plus fans cheering in the stadium.

## ONE SIMPLE THING

Complex adaptive systems are all around us, and though you may not pay much attention to them in your day-to-day interactions, they represent a model for how to think about the world. A **System** is a group of individuals or parts that interact and form an identifiable whole, such as your county's planning and zoning board. **Complex** means there is a diversity of parts that are interconnected, interdependent, and continually acting and reacting to what is happening around them and each other. There is a great deal of behind-the-scenes maneuvering going on by interested parties in anticipation of the upcoming vote on the new bond issue. **Adaptive** means being ready and able to change as circumstances change. It has just been reported that the date for the vote has been postponed due to the shifting political winds. People are responding to this latest decision by preparing for what will happen next.

Navigating within complex adaptive systems requires an understanding of systems dynamics, specifically the relationships and dependencies. Picture yourself driving on US Interstate Highway 5 in San Diego, California. Traffic flows in a choreographed routine, and those patterns of movement are in sync with the time of day, weather, road conditions, and others traveling alongside you. Up ahead there is a crash — conditions shift, and a new routine or pattern emerges. Six lanes of cars must gradually meld into two. In your rearview mirror you see a driver racing up behind you, illegally passing on the service road, and ready to cut in front of you. Every decision and action taken will affect others. Will you yield?

Whatever you decide, your actions contribute to, support, and influence the whole. This can be seen in all of the above examples. The ebb and

## Chapter 2. Think Systems

flow of energy, theories, plans, proposals, decisions, connections, and physical phenomena, among many other factors, shift the system and create its unpredictability. It is what also accounts for new ideas, structures, boundaries, philosophy, policy, inspiration or uncertainty to emerge. Bumps in the road and other random cosmic hiccups within systems give birth to original, exhilarating, and unprecedented occurrences.

The growing body of knowledge in the study of complex adaptive systems, and the theory and application of complexity science, gives us endless possibilities for understanding and influencing the world. The innovative discipline of Human Systems Dynamics has emerged from the exploration of the new sciences, and offers an exciting array of important concepts and tools to leverage the uncertainty around us. Founded by Dr. Glenda Eoyang, Human Systems Dynamics (HSD) uses vigorous metaphors, methods, and models that help individuals, communities, and organizations make sense of what is going on around them, including their own behavior. Many of those approaches provide the foundation for the work of this book.

Within everyday disorder and commotion, you can see and recognize patterns you, others, and society create. These patterns are the result of each and every interaction, circumstance, behavior, thought, and belief. The field of Human Systems Dynamics presents an exciting opportunity for learning and awareness, and identifying solutions that have long evaded us.

Still it is not enough to simply see; opportunity lies in making sense of that information, and then understanding what it means for you. Through her work in HSD, Dr. Eoyang defines and clarifies complex adaptive systems in this way: as *open, nonlinear,* and *high dimension*. As you think about these criteria, be sure to note where you see opportunities to learn and explore these ideas for yourself.

- **Open.** Open systems continuously interact with and respond to the environment. This leaves the system reliant on and potentially vulnerable to the unknown and unpredictable. When the temperature in your local neighborhood drops unexpectedly, everyone wears warm coats, hats, gloves, and scarves to watch the soccer game. Even an open system, however, with many diverse individuals and parts interacting in countless ways, must be bound. For example, your body is an open system, subject to external conditions, like exposure to cold germs or poison ivy. You also understand where your fingers end and your mittens begin.

Complex adaptive systems may be open and also embedded in other complex systems. The muscles and bones of your hand are part of your body; your body is part of a classroom; the classroom is part of a school, community, state, and so on. You can certainly imagine how one part or agent within a system (student, teacher or parent) can influence their own or other systems in the course of a day.

- **_Nonlinear._** There is an ongoing flow of energy into, out of, and throughout the system; and you learn from every act, experience, notion, and nuance. What you discovered yesterday influences your actions and decisions today; what you learn today may have an impact tomorrow or the next day, or not. The conversations you had with your mother years ago influence your interactions every day with your daughter; and the conversations you have with your daughter today will influence you for days and years to come – perhaps when you least expect it.

When you think about linearity, you think of events or actions moving in a straight line or in one direction: A leads to B and B leads to C. You slept through your alarm and arrived at work an hour late. Arriving an hour late for work, you missed the early-morning team meeting.

In this instance, as in a controlled laboratory environment, you can see with some degree of certainty the cause-and-effect relationship. In other words, two events occur in a particular order, and the second event is the result, consequence, or expected follow-up to the first event.

## Chapter 2. Think Systems

On the other hand, when your six-year-old niece pinches her four-year-old brother and runs into the next room for cover, the event may or may not have been predictable. He was sitting quietly and playing with his cars in the moments before she swooped in. And the effects of her action could also last beyond the tears and scolding that immediately follow. Or think about your career path: one thing can and often does lead to another, but frequently not in the ways you anticipated. The concept of starting and staying with one company for your entire career and working your way up the organizational ladder on a straight path from the mail room to the corner office, is no longer the norm or expectation. Or the phone in your backpack rings; who knows who or what is on the other end.

- **High dimension**. A complex adaptive system consists of many parts, many variables, many issues, and many choices. There are numerous elements or factors to consider, and each has the ability to influence the individual as well as the whole. Picture yourself standing on Main Street in a small town in any state, province or country. While there are several warm and friendly places to go for dinner, your options in town are few and therefore influence your choices for your evening out. This down-to-earth, uncomplicated scene may be quite appealing to you.

Now picture yourself standing in the center of a vibrant, international city anywhere across the globe. Far beyond gender, race, age, and culture, you will hear multiple dialects of multiple languages, and have endless options for education, learning, exploring the arts, and dining out. Think about music and theatre, universities, career opportunities, emergency rooms, perspectives, architecture, corporations, politics, media, and worldviews. Think about the types of restaurants in New York City, types of Italian restaurants in New York City, the types of Italian restaurants in one neighborhood in New York City. Hand-in-hand with infinite choices, ideas, sights, sounds, and ways of connecting with the world, is the recognition and appreciation that each of these parts, aspects, agents, entities, factors, and choices also influence the whole. A tragic fire in a local nightclub leads to new policies, laws, and safety regulations. A bitter election campaign produces a memorable sound bite, which sparks a local protest that grows into the Occupy Wall Street movement.

You are an integral part of these complex adaptive systems; and this book offers you a glimpse of and entry point into human systems dynamics, complexity, and systems thinking. My intention here is to provide a context and foundational understanding of how each individual – including YOU – has the potential to influence the whole.

One of the most intriguing aspects of complex systems is that when you rub against the current boundaries, frameworks, and elements of the system, you do not know exactly what will emerge.

The opportunity to sift through the potential is exhilarating. There is no right or wrong; your task is simply to seek the right combination of factors that make sense to you. Each of us needs to be able to play in the possibilities. As you, too, continue to recognize and appreciate the implications of your own behaviors, thoughts, and decision-making, you will gain more and more self-awareness and insights about YOU.

When you begin to Think Systems, it is easy to imagine how One Simple Thing can lead to another – and recognize the potential to create change in everything you do.

 **Simple Things to Consider:**

- Realizing we are connected and part of something – perhaps everything – else helps us appreciate our interdependencies and reliance on

## Chapter 2. Think Systems

others. What is an example of this dynamic in your own life when it comes to your own relationships and connections?

- We are part of families, neighborhoods, teams, companies, social groups, and communities bound together by common ideas, beliefs, and perspectives. In other words, we are part of countless open, nonlinear, and high dimension systems. Identify three systems you are part of. How do these systems overlap or connect? What is similar or different about each of these systems?

- What are three systems you are definitely not part of? How do you know?

# MADDY

*My deadline is fast approaching. At last and with a great leap of faith, I finally sit down at the computer to capture the thoughts and words that have been tumbling around in my head for weeks. It is before dawn and my mind is pushed to its weary edge. No matter when I receive the assignment for an article or story, it seems I cannot put pen to paper – or more accurately fingers to keyboard – until the very last minute. The editorial clock is relentlessly ticking away.*

*Picture the furious tap-tap-tapping in those last hours, when I think I cannot possibly finish in time. Imagine the recriminations: Why do I continue to do this? I must be self-destructive. My procrastination will be the end of me!*

*Suddenly, my brain erupts. Ideas and letters crash onto the page, and low and behold it not only makes sense but it is VERY GOOD! 'Tis a mystery whose answer lies within me.*

*More importantly, it is done. There is the payoff, but is it worth it?*

## ONE SIMPLE THING

*In those delicious moments when I have completed my final rewrite and punched the SEND key, I take a deep breath and virtuously pat myself on the back. I vow this is the last time. I will never, NEVER again wait until the last minute to buckle down and do it.*

*From here on, I will start early, step back, think, revise, finish, and submit my piece with plenty of time to spare. There will be no more headaches or fatigue, growling at everyone within one hundred yards, all-nighters, or self-rebuke. I have learned my lesson.*

*Until next time.*

# Chapter 3. Patterns

Individuals see, understand, and adapt to the world around them. A baby wants attention and discovers that by crying or gurgling or throwing a toy just out of reach, Mommy will respond. A toddler recognizes that when he falls and scrapes his knee, if Grandpa is nearby, crying elicits a warm embrace and soothing sounds. If Grandpa has gone to get his glasses, then the best thing to do is get up, brush off the dirt, and keep going. A teenager can anticipate Dad's response when he breaks curfew, as well as when he brings home a first-rate report card. And an understanding mom knows when her daughter has had an argument with her boyfriend with one perceptive glance.

What this all points to is an awareness that your experiences, great and small, and the people around you contribute to shaping your thoughts, actions, behaviors, and decisions. You create patterns and/or respond to the patterns around you, often without even being aware of their existence. It is no coincidence that long-married couples can finish each others' sentences or anticipate a partner's moods. And no wonder your kid sister can always manage to push your hot buttons and set you off. She helped create and continues to reinforce your patterns, and her own. Yes, these are the patterns that surround you.

## ONE SIMPLE THING

Consciously or not, a child understands that there is no point in crying if no one is there to hear and respond. Cringing when your in-laws come for a visit is your default reaction because of the patterns that began and have continued in your relationship since the first time their son introduced you. And when you get home from work, cross and unhappy because your boss does not "have your back" when you need his support, your partner always manages to have a warm embrace and your favorite comfort food waiting for you.

You see the world as you are, rather than how it might really be; and you make sense of what is around you – by learning and adapting. Specifically, that means shifting your patterns. I recently overheard someone say, "I always wind up with the wrong mates." I thought about that admission and wondered about her patterns in romantic relationships. What was it, now and in the past, that set up that repeating, damaging dynamic? It did not sound like she enjoyed the relationships she found herself in; yet they persisted. What was she doing to reinforce and maintain them?

Cathy, a longtime friend and colleague, likes to say, "Once is a blip; twice is a coincidence; and three times is a pattern." With that in mind, take a moment right now and think about some of the everyday patterns that exist around you. For example,

- What is your morning routine?
- Who has lunch with whom at the office?
- What does a typical weekend at your house look like?
- How do you unwind after a taxing day?
- What are your favorite pastimes?
- How do you respond when someone asks you for help?

Consider this: within a particular context or set of circumstances, you conduct yourself in a specific way. Your behavior is proactive or reactive, positive or negative, enthusiastic and joyful or petulant and whiny. These

## Chapter 3. Patterns

behaviors then create patterns. How you respond in certain, many, or all situations, is based upon your knowledge, understanding, and expectations. These patterns in turn create your *"SELF"*: the sum total of your experiences, education, beliefs, feelings, choices, and relationships. An awareness of your patterns is an awareness of your identity. In other words, your patterns produce who you are when you talk about YOU.

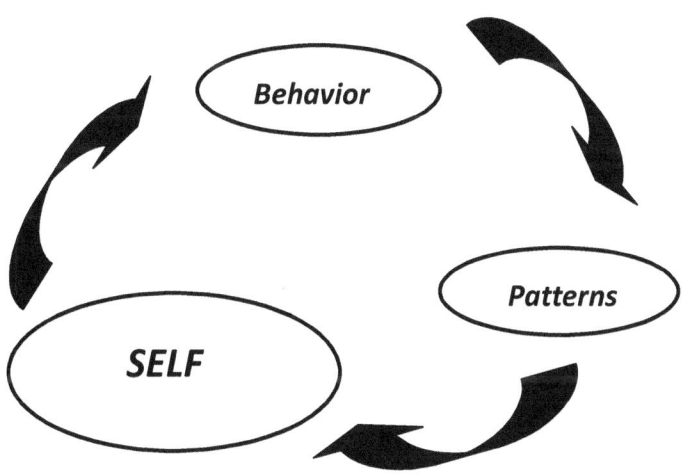

This composite of yourself then reinforces your behaviors and strengthens your patterns, which further supports who you are, and so on. And this circular process is ongoing unless or until you change your behavior and do something different – just One Simple Thing. Once your behavior shifts, you have begun to alter your patterns. And when your patterns shift, you change. Therefore, it is YOU who decide, and YOU who can influence this process.

The next time your sister tries to provoke you, respond in a new way, laugh it off, or don't respond at all. Shift your behavior and create a new pattern. It may take more than one attempt to change this familiar scenario, but it will be worth it. If doing the same thing yields the same results then do something different and watch what happens.

## AMP and DAMP

So the question is this: are your patterns working for you? After all, you don't often stop to think about what is going on; it just is. Your patterns, like habits and regular routines, have become so ingrained that they are quite natural and fixed in the course of your day. Or are they? Perhaps it is time to start fine-tuning your actions and use your ability to **AMP** and **DAMP.**

Are you satisfied, relieved, content, optimistic, feeling powerful, managing in times of stress, and able to accomplish what you need to do when you need to do it? Are your relationships positive and productive, your times at work and play rewarding and full of enjoyment and meaning? Is what you are doing personally and professionally aligned with your beliefs, values, and goals? Do you fit with the environment and flow of the world around you?

If so, now is the time to think about how you can enhance, increase and *amplify* those patterns so that you are not merely maintaining the status quo but boosting your energy, enthusiasm, and physical, emotional, and spiritual self. Like Judy.

*Recently Judy reached out to a group of improvisational players at the local community theatre. Several weeks ago, a conversation triggered a rush of memories from college and she recalled how much she had enjoyed her involvement with the theatre studies department. It was a time of discovery, inventiveness, imagination, fun, and laughter. Judy immersed herself in the work – even though it was hard work, she loved it! – and was rewarded by a boost in confidence, a keen sense of belonging, bringing something*

## Chapter 3. Patterns

*new to fruition with colleagues, and developing a strong sense of self-awareness. Judy knows she cannot recreate a magical time from her past, but there is no reason she cannot start anew in a familiar setting and experience again the satisfaction and connections she once enjoyed. Focusing on an activity that had previously offered an opportunity to reach out, explore, and connect, Judy **amp**ed the patterns that worked best for her.*

Or are your patterns hindering you? Are you restless, anxious, at your wits' end, dissatisfied, tired, feeling powerless, impatient, finding fault, feeling afraid, and out-of-sync with what is important to you? Are you conscious of a lack of fit between you and your world?

If so, now is the time to think about how you can diminish, decrease, shift, dispel, disperse, and **dampen** those patterns so that you can discover exactly what is important to you, righting what appears to be wrong, and shifting your practice to what will work best for you. Like Cal.

*Cal rediscovered running while in the service overseas. Running, like most athletic endeavors, brings together a community of like-minded men and women. Cal definitely enjoyed working out with a group, and the social time that often followed. Yes, he appreciated the times he ran alone, with his own thoughts keeping him company; however, it was both comfortable and challenging to keep up with the rhythmic pace of other runners. Several weeks ago a few members of the group decided to start rating and ranking each other for fun. "Friendly competition," folks said affably. "Let's make this interesting." Well, it did not take long for the competition to turn grim and all sorts of hidden agendas emerged. Cal began to take his morning runs too seriously, which set off his whole day. By the time he arrived at the office he was feeling dissatisfied and irritable. People certainly noticed and as far as Cal was concerned, this was definitely not working anymore. It* was time for Cal to refocus, shift, and **damp** the counterproductive patterns that had emerged over time.

## FITNESS

Beyond a good fit, you are looking for *fitness*. Fitness, of course, conjurers up images of athletes, endless laps around the track, and being able to qualify for a national sporting or endurance event. But there is another kind of fitness: how you participate in your own life, the decisions you make, and the thoughts and actions that shout out who you are, what's important to you, and how you want to be in the world.

**Fitness** *is the alignment of you with your world, and the world making sense to you. It exemplifies a solid coherence of your values, beliefs, and how you live day-to-day.*

Your fitness centers on being acutely aware of those things that have made you the person you are and will continue to become. It is the indicator of physical, emotional, and spiritual understanding and well-being, recognizing that which constitutes positive or negative factors in your life.

This means acknowledging and living according to a set of guidelines and ideas that speak to your core; how you develop and build satisfied and functioning relationships and connections near and far, and then growing into your best self.

## Chapter 3. Patterns

This book is about creating believable change. That change must resonate with who you are, and empower you to carefully examine your patterns and decide what you are going to do about your life. Are your patterns helping or hurting you day-to-day in your actions, thoughts, and decisions, spurring you on or blocking your way? Using your skills, talents, experience, and what you know and will learn about yourself, it's time to stand in a space of inquiry and ask yourself the following questions.

- **What do you want to achieve?** There are many sound answers to this question, and as you are starting to pay attention to the patterns around you, there may be some Aha's along the way as you think about your responses. For example, your first response may be, "I want a promotion." Before you move on to the next question, pause and explore for just a moment what that means. Do you want more responsibility? Do you want to be doing something different, more exciting, and with more interactions with your peers? Do you want a raise in salary, and an office with a door and two windows? Do you want to make a larger contribution to your organization in a more meaningful role? Do you want to be the boss? All of these and more may be pieces of the answer to the question, "What do you want to achieve?"

- **What benefits are you seeking?** You may not be the only one who will reap the rewards of your efforts. Your desire to create change and strengthen your own capacity can also be about supporting others. Coaching your son's softball team can be fun AND bring the two of you closer together. Purpose and meaning may, indeed, be what you are after. Equally valid are a shorter work week, and more free time to improve your tennis serve.

- **Are you paying attention to what is going on around you?** In open, high dimension, and nonlinear systems, there is a confluence of movement at all times, and something is always happening. Context, environments, perspectives, timing, and priorities shift along with the flow of information and energy. So what will that mean for you? Is your job being relocated? Are you getting ready for an empty nest or preparing for a grown "boomerang" son to return to your nest? Will you be taking care of elderly parents? Is the current economic forecast positive or negative? How will these or other events and circumstances influence your choices?

- **What strengths do you have to build on?** Start from where you are. Recognize your individual capabilities – your knowledge, skills, commitment, perspective, resilience, and the will to make a difference – and then continue from there.

- **How will you be creating this change; what will you need to do?** Implicit in this question and beyond a prescribed schedule or To-Do list, is knowing when and where and how your activities will be implemented, supported, and sustained. Timing may be a critical element, and your pursuits may focus on your personal or professional life, the decisions of others, and more. What will you also need from others to be successful?

- **What is it about this process/method and doing it right now that will make the difference?** In addition to your own personal readiness, this method is grounded in and builds upon solid theory and practice of human systems dynamics and complexity science. You will recognize relationships between actions and outcomes, and you will see how a collection of specific activities – driven by YOU and for YOU – can lead to the unfolding of complex change over time. You will be watching the various moving parts on your map, and as you learn and use the tools offered here, you will practice and gather your own strength and resiliency.

*You Can Do This!*

## Chapter 3. Patterns

Sometimes change is less about particular causes, than events or the conditions that are present at a moment in time.

In open, high dimension, and nonlinear complex adaptive systems, there may be nothing akin to a direct cause and effect or straight-line link between occurrences; however as the system's dynamics shift, conditions are altered and opportunities emerge. At the community level, for example, the unexpected restructuring of a leading university foundation may create conditions conducive to changes in policy, procedures, protocols and/or practices for students, staff, faculty, and the local population at large. If you are among any of these groups, this could be your time to act.

For you, your own circumstances in particular may include any or all of the following.

- A growing dissatisfaction and divide between what is important to you and what you are actually doing.
- An environment of fixed and unyielding barriers that deny diversity of perspective, thought, or action.
- A scarcity of learning, growth, integrity, and meaning, in the moment or over time.
- A problem you have been working on for some time suddenly yielding a new or different result because of a shift in perspective, an unpredictable event, or a new addition to the environment.

*You want to intentionally change your life. Well, it's all about patterns – your own, and the patterns around you.*

Like many other things, patterns come in all shapes and sizes, colors, and stripes. There are patterns of permission, patterns of confidence, patterns of loyalty, patterns of approval, patterns of doing what you are told and by whom, patterns of risk and exploration, patterns of work and play, patterns of music and prose. These represent just a scant few, but you get the idea.

If you are prepared to open up to new ideas, insights, and understanding about yourself, and if you are ready to be changed in the process of creating change, now is the time. Start with this One Simple Thing:

**Take a few moments to think about your own patterns and then in the space below, identify one pattern you would like to AMP and one pattern you would like to DAMP.**

---

I would like to **amp**:

I would like to **damp**:

---

Now imagine what those changes might look like as you take a giant step toward creating and living your own Theory of Change.

## Chapter 3. Patterns

 **Simple Things to Consider:**

- How do the patterns of behavior of someone else in your life support or undermine your own patterns?

- What would fitness look like for you?

## MALLARY

Looking back, I see how fortunate I was to have experienced a fairly traditional, ingenuous, and "programmed" upbringing. There were the typical expectations and givens presented to girls like me: middle class, second-generation American, living in New York City, and coming of age in the 1960s and 1970s. Ours was a safe and reasonably diverse neighborhood, its greatest strength being its familiar, common ground. The prevailing pattern: everyone looked out for each other.

Like many kids, I walked to and from my elementary school – seven blocks each way – knowing that our highly networked community was filled with treats and traps. Treat: my grandparents, who adored me, lived in the middle of my route home, and I would often stop after school for a piece of freshly baked coffee cake and a glass of warm, milky coffee. Trap: if I was doing anything even remotely suspicious, our stalwart neighbor Lily, halfway down the street and always stationed at her second-floor apartment window, was on the telephone with my mother before my first turn.

# ONE SIMPLE THING

*There were plenty of rules growing up, and as I recall I now realize these were both the patterns and Simple Rules that bound our families, friends, and communities together.*

- *"Be good," my mom would sing out as I left for a friend's house or on a local shopping excursion. I thought everyone's mom said this, until the first time I called for a new girl in the neighborhood, and as we walked out her mom said solemnly, "Be wise." Wow!*
- *"Call if you're going to be late."*
- *"Wait till your father gets home!"*
- *"Respect your elders."*
- *And the ever-daunting, "Don't do anything I wouldn't do." What exactly did that mean, anyway?*

*These notions, however, set the conditions for a life filled with choices, opportunities, connections, patterns, and inquiry.*

# Chapter 4. Radical Inquiry and Simple Rules

I trust Simple Rules. They provide a straightforward, intuitive, and uncomplicated set of guidelines for living. They are comprised of what you believe and understand about yourself, offering a common focal point for who you are, what is important to you, and how you want to connect with others.

When we wrote the book *Simple Rules: A Radical Inquiry into Self* (Gold Canyon Press, 2009), Royce Holladay and I began this journey – and much of the discussion included here in this chapter about Simple Rules and Radical Inquiry is gleaned from that book.

At that time we sought to create an in-depth understanding of complex systems, mapping out a path toward discovering and building coherence in our lives and the systems we inhabit. We talked about Radical Inquiry as a process of introspection and self-discovery; Simple Rules, based upon one's own values and beliefs, allow one to create a personal framework to guide thinking, decision-making, and behavior.

I do not intend to restate or rewrite that book here, but to offer a recap of both Simple Rules and Radical Inquiry as foundational pieces for your own work.

And if you have not already done so, *Simple Rules* might be a worthwhile read.

# ONE SIMPLE THING

**RADICAL INQUIRY**

The concept of Radical Inquiry emerged in 2004 when a group of dedicated practitioners came together through the Human Systems Dynamics Institute to explore complexity and complex adaptive systems. Our objective was to develop and compile a body of research, resources, and rigorous protocols from practitioners and for practitioners working in the field. Since then, the original concept has evolved into a model of reflection and exploration, helping to set conditions for understanding oneself. The following explanation is from the book *Simple Rules*.

***Inquiry** is the act of asking questions and believing the answers are not already known. To stand in inquiry is to go past what you think you know, and to seek authenticity. It is to allow yourself to be wrong, to be surprised, and see the world in new ways. Living in inquiry is to live in the questions that help you understand your life and your world. There are always going to be questions – even about yourself – where you don't know the answers. What this means is answers are knowable and within you, waiting to be discovered.*

***Radical?** Yes, because it requires you to ask basic and powerful questions about the roots – the radical core – of your life. Beyond even your own thoughtful introspection, Radical Inquiry engages and induces you to explore the very essence of who you are and what your self is about. You are now digging into and unearthing your own foundation.*

This process is about discovering you, and you've probably been asking yourself the following questions or others similar to them for some time now.

## Chapter 4. Radical Inquiry and Simple Rules

- What do I want to spend my days doing?
- What makes me smile?
- What do I like thinking, learning, and talking about?
- What kind of environment do I find supportive, empowering, and encouraging?
- What inspires me most?
- What do I most enjoy?
- What motivates me to do my best?
- Which causes do I believe in and connect with?
- Given what I know about myself, how can I make a contribution to the greater good?

These questions and your responses speak to your quest for the life that nourishes, supports, and fits you. In addition, certain patterns have no doubt emerged from your responses. For example, when you think about the perfect environment for yourself, what do you see? What pattern emerges when you focus on the contributions you make to your family and community? When you make important decisions do you consider your needs and wants, and what are the patterns that emerge from those areas of your life?

Recognizing and understanding your patterns is a good place to start this work.

Radical Inquiry simplifies this process by asking just three simple questions. They are straightforward, less complicated, and as you will see, run throughout this book.

- *Who are you?*
- *What's important to you?*
- *How do you want to connect with others and the world?*

# ONE SIMPLE THING

Begin to think about your answers. Start by identifying a desired outcome or particular area on which you want to focus. For example, your desired outcome might be:

*Making a Real Difference for Youth in My Community*

The broad nature of this outcome allows for flexibility, weighing a diversity of ideas, and then zooming in on a particular objective. With that in mind, identify one particular aspect of your goal, such as *changing local policy on the availability and use of recreation space for teens after school.*

Begin with a drawing of three overlapping circles, or Venn diagram, as pictured below. You see that each circle contains one of the Radical Inquiry questions and in the very center is a star. The star represents your desired outcome.

**Starting with the star in the center, write your particular area of focus in that space.**

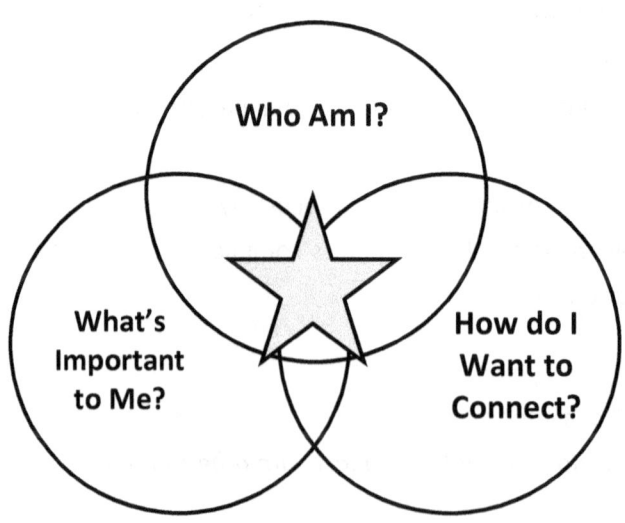

## Chapter 4. Radical Inquiry and Simple Rules

**Who are you?** What is your response to the question in the top circle? There are, of course, many answers to this question, and some are certainly grounded in where you are and what you are doing at any given moment in time. Stay centered on the particular slice of the overall goal you wish to tackle. For example, beyond the obvious, (woman, mom, sister, professional), you could also choose learner, mentor, ally, mediator, coach, contributor, activist. None are wrong; you just have to decide what is appropriate for you in this context. ***Write your answers in the circle.***

**What is important to you?** For the lower left circle, think about what factors, concepts, values or beliefs stand out for you and remain a priority in this specific area of your life. What influences important decisions you make? It could be access to resources; learning new skills that can be shared; fair opportunities; or anything else that resonates with you. ***In that circle, write down your responses to the question.***

**How do you want to connect with others?** To complete the lower right circle, how will you engage or connect with others? Will you advocate for your cause, or be an active, present listener? Will you use the power of technology and expanded community networks to speak, listen, motivate, inspire, provide feedback, measure, and change your community? What are the words that will fill that space and have meaning for you? ***Write your responses in the third circle.***

When you are done, think about what your responses say about you. There will be emerging patterns in your words and ideas. Are your answers true and useful to you? Does what you have written make sense? Pay particular attention to the areas where the questions and your responses overlap; is what you believe about yourself consistent with what you are seeing? Is there alignment between what you believe and your desired outcome? Does what you have written do justice to and accurately reflect your ideas and commitment? Does it fit? Good!

*If your answer is No, revisit your responses to find the separation or disconnect between what you have written and what you believe to be true. Your answers should be consistent and coherent with your desired outcome, as well as your values and beliefs.*

It is important to note that you can approach your Radical Inquiry from two perspectives. The first is this: start by saying, "Right now this is the current situation. It is not working for me and in order to create change I want to amplify some patterns, dampen or eliminate others, and/or create altogether new ones that will be a better fit. Hence my responses and desired patterns represent those areas where I want to make a change, based upon what I know and believe."

The second approach is to start with a clean slate and say, "This is what I aspire to and want to build from scratch. I want to forget about or disregard what came before – I want to begin anew and create exactly those patterns that best fit me starting now."

From either stance, be open to the possibilities, the unpredictable, and the unexpected. That is why this is called Radical Inquiry. Remember, the answers you have given are your own; and the patterns you identified are the patterns you want to create.

And as stated previously, don't be surprised to see these three simple questions – *Who are you? What is important to you?* and *How do you want to connect with others?* – repeated throughout this book. These simple questions are incredibly powerful and will remain touchstones for you as you are moving forward.

## Chapter 4. Radical Inquiry and Simple Rules

 **Simple Things to Consider:**

- Where two circles/questions overlap in the diagram, what patterns would you expect to see from your combined responses?

- Once you have created the change you want for yourself, what would be the same and what would be different?

- What surprises emerged from your Radical Inquiry?

## SIMPLE RULES

Imagine you are on vacation, looking forward to a day of deep-sea fishing off the Florida coast. As your captain heads for the recommended fishing grounds, you watch the waves move past and the shore recede behind you. You lazily consider what you might catch today and notice the birds overhead following the boat. Every so often you see a dark triangle break the water's surface. It is a shark fin, and you begin to wonder about sharks in these waters.

Right now, take a moment to reflect. What would you say, in a few simple words or phrases, about how sharks exist, day-to-day, in the oceans? Well, even if all you know about sharks was learned from the National Geographic Channel, how about this:

- Maintain forward motion, or keep swimming.
- Feed to capacity, or keep eating.
- Reproduce offspring, or keep having baby sharks.

In fact, this verbal image was presented with authority to me and my classmates by a tour guide, during a school field trip to the New York Aquarium. Years later I realized it was a terrific list of Simple Rules for Sharks, and it has stuck with me.

Of course, there is no empirical data to show that sharks hold to any such list of rules, and the lack of concrete evidence leads some individuals to reject the idea of Simple Rules completely. Where these concepts can apply, and in fact prove valuable and effective, is in human systems. They are wonderful metaphors for exploring and explaining individual and group behaviors.

*Simple Rules* are a set of guidelines based upon your values and beliefs, and the conditions you set to shape the patterns of your life. They are the foundation for how you think and act.

The concept of Simple Rules emerged from the work of researchers and technicians who used computer simulations to study animal behavior in natural environments. For example, how do herding animals gather and travel together in the amazing ways they do, or how do indigenous populations migrate over time? In 1986, researcher Craig Reynolds first developed BOIDS, an "artificial-life" program, which enabled him to examine live systems using computer models and robotics. What emerged were repeating patterns of birds flocking, and a short list of Simple Rules.

With all of this in mind, think about the "real-life" program in your own neighborhood. Imagine what would happen If everyone in your community believed in and acted upon the Simple Rule, "Respect your elders." What are the types of recognizable and characteristic patterns you would see? Or, if in your company, collaboration and teamwork provided the core of your Simple Rules, you would find yourself in an environment where trust and mutual support were the order of the day. From this perspective,

## Chapter 4. Radical Inquiry and Simple Rules

behaviors of people—either in groups or individually—are shaped by their own short lists of Simple Rules.

By the way, Simple Rules exist whether we are aware of them or not, whether or not we even explicitly recognize them. For example, imagine you were a fly buzzing around your office throughout your typical work day. What would you see, what patterns would emerge, and what would you think about it all? You would, no doubt, see the existing Simple Rules in effect, guiding what was happening in any one moment, as well as over time. These might be dysfunctional patterns of gossip, absenteeism, and favoritism. Or, you might see productive patterns of team spirit, cooperation, mentoring, and coaching of employees by their supervisors.

*Like it or not, Simple Rules and their corresponding patterns are there.*

Once you begin to pay attention, you will notice how patterns change along with slight alterations in the Rules. For example, let's suppose a new team supervisor has been hired in your department. The previous manager believed in a strict adherence to punctuality above all else. One of his Simple Rules was, "Be on time." Your new supervisor cares more about results than the time clock. One of her Simple Rules is, "Pay attention to quality and results." As different patterns of behavior began to form, those ripples would be felt in both predictable and unpredictable ways, and could potentially create a huge shift in the overall pattern of the organization.

The same applies to you. Imagine how changing your own Simple Rules can help you change your own patterns of behavior in both expected and unexpected ways. A short list of Simple Rules allows you to get back to basics, and create a context and framework for what you value.

When it comes time to make a decision, Simple Rules are the playbook for your next move. Because of the nature of Simple Rules, they are broad enough to fit into any context, yet unambiguous enough to be clear. For example, "Ask questions" may sound like a simple learning instruction when trying to understand a new concept or shopping for an electronic gadget. And it is – but it can also be a metaphor for how you proceed down the road when entering unfamiliar territory. Do you embrace learning and growth as an opportunity to grasp insights, expand your consciousness and horizons, and discover new prospects? Do you gather all the information you need before you make a decision? Do you thoroughly weigh your options before making a decision and look at things from multiple vantage points? Are you sure that nothing has been omitted or overlooked? And are you prepared for unpredictable or changing circumstances, potential dangers, safety concerns, and reliance on the actions and abilities of others? In other words, have you collected all the data, made meaning of it, and then decided you are ready to act?

One of the Simple Rules growing up in my family was, "Complete your education." No matter what, college was not an option – it was a given, carefully planned for, and as straightforward as any responsibility we had. Education was one of the most fundamental requirements in our house, and throughout my childhood, I pictured myself standing on the brink of something wondrous, clutching my diploma in my hand, ready to set out into the world.

But learning and growth are never-ending, so does one ever actually finish their education? I do not think I will ever complete mine, and I do not mind one bit.

The metaphor and application here support the notion that there is learning in every instance, no matter how old you are or whether you will be graded. Be open to it; embrace it; and be grateful for it.

*Remember that your Simple Rules are about you and yourself. They may be very different from someone else's – even diametrically opposed. And yes, it is hard to suspend judgment from this process when you want to change the world for the good. By focusing on influencing patterns and*

## Chapter 4. Radical Inquiry and Simple Rules

*behaviors, you are able to exercise your significant power to influence, and hopefully turn judgment aside.*

What are YOUR Simple Rules? Think about that fly buzzing about, observing you at home and at work, in your everyday interactions and over time. What would the fly see, based upon what you believe and value, the patterns you wish to create, and your Radical Inquiry? Alternatively, what would you like your Simple Rules to be, from this moment forward?

***After taking some time to reflect, use the space below to begin creating your own short list of Simple Rules. Try to come up with two or three as a starting point for yourself; or use this opportunity to revisit Simple Rules you already have. Be sure to start your Simple Rules with a verb because Simple Rules are about action.***

**My Short List of Simple Rules:**

→

→

# ONE SIMPLE THING

→

→

→

→

Hint: If this is your first time identifying your Simple Rules, know that this process can take quite a bit of time. You may also come up with a list, put it aside and come back to it after you have had some time and space to think about your choices. Remember there are no right or wrong answers. What is right or wrong is what is right or wrong for you. Go ahead and live with your Simple Rules for a while and see how they fit. If they are not quite right you can review and/or amend your list. It is a good idea to revisit your short list of Simple Rules regularly anyway – things change, and you will, too.

 **Simple Things to Consider:**

About a year ago, a colleague of mine from the Netherlands shared the following with a group of us during an online discussion about complexity, conditions for creating change, and Simple Rules.

*"We have a piano at the public library in Amsterdam. There is a simple rule displayed prominently on it: 'Only play this instrument if you know how to.' What do we think?"*

I thought about this Simple Rule and decided I liked it. My reasoning was as follows:

If you only do what you are told and allow others to define the parameters, constrain your action, or limit the possibilities, then you may indeed only sit down at the piano when you "know how to." And if you have had piano lessons when you were a child, like I did, you would feel comfortable and at liberty to tinkle the keyboard. Yet you might not, if you are feeling a bit rusty. So this might indeed seem to be simply an instruction within a single circumstance.

On the other hand, if perhaps you are looking to change your patterns, or create new ones, I see this as a delightfully scalable (no pun intended) and practical way of exploring and expanding goals, priorities, possibilities,

## ONE SIMPLE THING

potential, behavior, AND patterns. This might be your Simple Rule; particularly if you are clear about who you are, what is important to you, and how you want to connect with others and the world.

As a metaphor for living, *"Only play this instrument if you know how to"* says the following to me.

- Move forward if you have examined the situation, are confident you know what to do, what you are capable of doing, and are ready to act.
- Go on and take that risk (chance, job, opportunity, etc.) if you have calculated the costs and benefits, and understand the implications and rewards of your actions.
- If you recognize that nothing is guaranteed or completely predictable in this world, and you are willing to accept that, dive right in.
- And remember on occasion to push pause and reflect on where you are headed. Once you have analyzed what you see and what you know, you can make an informed decision, and then proceed.

For me, the opportunities to see, understand, and exercise my ability and will to influence the situation lie in the following questions.

- What do I know (about playing the piano or ...?)
- So what does that mean for me, and what will I decide (about playing this instrument or ...?)
- And now what will I do?

*So, what do YOU think?*

## *CARLA*

Carla has been a Resource Teacher in her school district for many years and though she has more than adequate savings to consider retirement, she wouldn't think of it. Carla prides herself on her commitment to her students and is generous with her time, energy, and money when it benefits local children and families. She is also devoted to her own family and appreciates the close relationship they enjoy. Carla takes care of her health and looks forward to being a vibrant part of her grandchildren's lives for many years to come.

Lately, Carla has become acutely aware of the increasing local needs: that there are people right here in her own city who do not have enough to eat; that there is a growing homeless population; that being unemployed is not always by your own choice; and that there are kids attending her own school who would benefit from having stable, supportive adults in their lives.

The more she thinks about it, the more she realizes she would like to help meet the needs of others right here in her community. She could make a difference and she truly believes the more she is able to give, the more she herself will receive.

# Chapter 5. Simple Tools

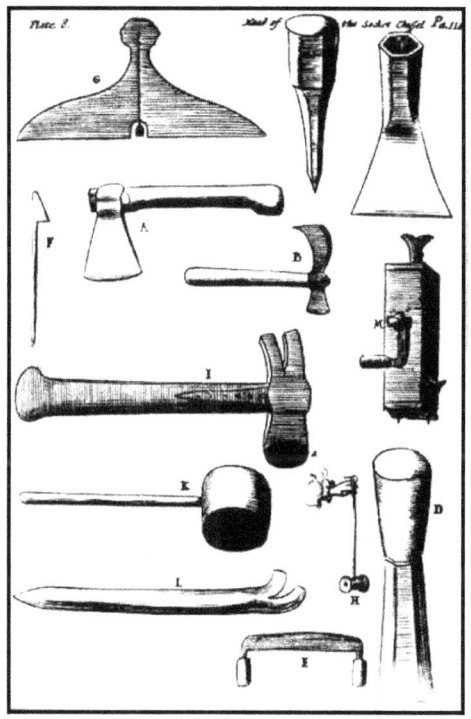

Smithsonian Collection

Human systems – people – are unlike other naturally occurring systems. After all, you have thoughts, opinions, judgments, memories, emotions, and imagination. These are grounded in: frames of reference and worldview; the nature of your relationships and how they develop and prosper; how you communicate and connect with the world; how you grow and share resources, ideas, and energy; and where you place your faith.

Because you can suppose, imagine, decide, and act upon your choices, you also have the extraordinary ability to influence your world. For example, you carry with you an individual set of lenses through which you see the world. This point of view includes pictures from your past, e.g. the neighborhood where you grew up, family and friends around you, and familiar sights, sounds, and smells; your own experiences and learning; and patterns developed over time. Every simple thing you do, action you take, or decision you make has the infinite potential of influencing everything else around you.

Even now, when collaborating with others, you form expectations about what is acceptable within your associations, what works for the general welfare of your communities, and what you aspire to create for today and tomorrow. You continue to build a life and a culture that is characterized by patterns of interaction and decision-making, and bound by your choices.

If you are looking to change your patterns, or create new ones, the Simple Tools presented in this chapter offer uncomplicated, down-to-earth ways of doing so by exploring and understanding yourself. Each tool builds upon the one before to help you identify, clarify, and refine your goals, priorities, outcomes, and patterns.

In open, complex environments, numerous activities, strategies, and systems dynamics are constants. The efficacy of actions and outcomes designed to support you in realizing your goals depends upon an accurate appraisal of your behavior, actions, and the environmental circumstances which support it. This process is highly participatory and focused – and all about YOU.

As you explore and practice these tools, remember that your decision-making is grounded in questions.

## Chapter 5. Simple Tools

- What are the patterns you want to generate through your change efforts?
- What are your indicators of success?
- Is what you are learning both true and useful to you?
- In a world filled with differences, what are the differences that make a difference?
- What are the conditions you need to create the patterns you want?

If you are aware of all these complexities and their entanglements, you can recognize and appreciate the need for new and different techniques – that attend to important interactions amidst competing interests and values in your environment – and techniques that are simple. By becoming familiar with and at ease with these tools, you will be able to discern, if not all the answers to your questions, at least the beginning of the right questions.

One more thing: these tools are here in service to your purpose, and are a means to an important end. That is, your best self. Recognize the tools as simply that.

### I. ADAPTIVE ACTION

When working in complex systems we need a methodology that allows us the openness and flexibility to deal with and understand what emerges; prepares us for the unknown; supports effective and sustainable decision-making and action; and allows individuals and communities to quickly shift. This is beyond being prepared: this is about being prepared to act, and then doing so.

*Meg, your good friend and colleague, has headed back home to see her dad who has been in a serious car crash. She will be staying with him for a while, and you've generously and readily agreed to take care of her cats and water the plants. All seems well; Dad will be coming home at the end of the week, and arrangements have been made for his physical therapy and long-term care while recuperating.*

*Unfortunately, the next time you arrive at Meg's house, you find the air conditioning has died and you need to rescue the kitties. After all, this is July and you live in Phoenix, Arizona. You take the cats home, and they are welcomed into your own brood. What is the best way to take care of the situation without distressing Meg any more than necessary?*

*Well, it's a good thing you know about "these things." The air conditioner still has a name plate attached with important manufacturer's information on it, as well as the date of purchase. You get in touch with the repairman, set up an appointment, and plan to take tomorrow afternoon off to meet him at Meg's. Now when you call her, you let her know all is in order, and you both breathe a sigh of relief. It turns out the compressor is under warranty and for about $200 – service call and labor – all is cool.*

You reviewed the information you had, made sense of it, formed a plan, and then did what you needed to do.

This is **Adaptive Action**: seeing, understanding, and then acting. The Adaptive Action Model was developed by Dr. Glenda Eoyang, and is the focus of the book *Adaptive Action: Leveraging Uncertainty in your Organization* (Eoyang and Holladay, Stanford University Press, 2013). This valuable tool provides an iterative process to plan for and bring about change, and then prepare for what is needed next. This allows for immediate feedback as each cycle is completed — measuring success and getting ready for your next opportunity.

Adaptive Action consists of three phases and questions, **What? So What?** and **Now What?**

## Chapter 5. Simple Tools

**What?** This first phase consists of collecting all the data at hand. In other words, what do you know about the situation? This will tell you the current state of affairs: what is happening right now, existing patterns and activities, and what has been accomplished so far. The information may come from multiple means: conversations, correspondence, personal observation, policy, performance measures, interviews, records, the skills, abilities, and knowledge of individuals, and so forth. Everything is data and specific questions for you here may include:

- What is the challenge?
- What is my role?
- What patterns do I see?
- What can I learn?
- What do I really need?

**So What?** In this phase you will look at the information you have and determine what it means in relation to your overall goal. In other words, what do you understand about what you know, and what are the implications for you and the whole based upon the data you have? Specific questions for you here may include:

- What patterns do I see/want to see?
- What more do I need to know?
- What are the potential implications of my actions?
- What do I need to do?
- What am I able to do to change the current situation?

**Now What?** This final phase addresses decisions and actions, with a focus on the overall target. Specific questions for you here may include:

- Now as I take action, what do I see happening?

- Is what I see what I wanted to see?
- What do I know that I did not know before?
- What do I need to do to change the situation?
- Now what do I do next?

These questions close the loop and bring you back to start the process all over again. Your actions have altered the environment and new information is available for you.

The story about Meg is a simple illustration of how you can see what's in front of you, make sense of it, and then act. If you think about it, you rely on this process almost constantly in your head as you appraise and act on any circumstance around you, weighing your options, and then making an informed decision.

Perhaps you have been offered a new job.

*What do you know?*

- There are expanded responsibilities.
- There will be significantly more compensation.
- The working hours will be longer.
- The commute to the new office will take almost twice as long in the morning.

*So What does it mean?*

- It is a giant step up on your career ladder.
- The money will help with your son's college tuition.
- You hate the thought of extra time on the road and fighting rush-hour traffic.

*Now What are you going to do?*

## Chapter 5. Simple Tools

- That's up to you, based upon what you know and the implications your decision has on your life, goals, beliefs, and values. You do, however, have lots of resources available to you for help. For example, go back to your Radical Inquiry and think about who you are, what is important to you, and how you want to connect with others around you. Revisit your Simple Rules and think about which decision will be coherent and consistent with your beliefs. And carefully consider Fit: will your decision support and help sustain your physical, emotional, and spiritual well-being?

The true value of Adaptive Action cannot be overstated:

- You are already using this tool. By slowing down and paying attention to the process, you can see why and how you respond in situations. While some decisions are mundane – you are out of chocolate ice cream so you will have strawberry ice cream instead – the opportunities to significantly influence your world are immense.

- You are presented with almost instant feedback, allowing you to begin to weigh your next options, and respond with an informed decision, based upon the review of new information, and its implications.

- When your mind is in sync with what is going on around you, the opportunity to understand the information before you, and view your options keeps you from getting stuck.

- One of the most critical benefits of using adaptive action is this: whenever you come face-to-face with a problem, you immediately want to identify a solution and act. Ours is a society that values and rewards action, the sooner the better. "This is what we know, now what are we going to do about it – and how fast?" This middle phase is where I believe you can have the most impact. Asking *So What?* provides an opportunity to tap on the brakes and say, "Whoa, not so fast. What does this all mean? What can be inferred for myself and others? What are my options, best case, and worst case? Let me take a minute (or ten), push pause, and think. And when I am done, then I can act."

This middle step also allows you to make more informed, thoughtful decisions. Your influence may be larger than you will ever know; it is worthwhile to take a breath, reflect, and then hit the gas. It is One Simple Thing you can do.

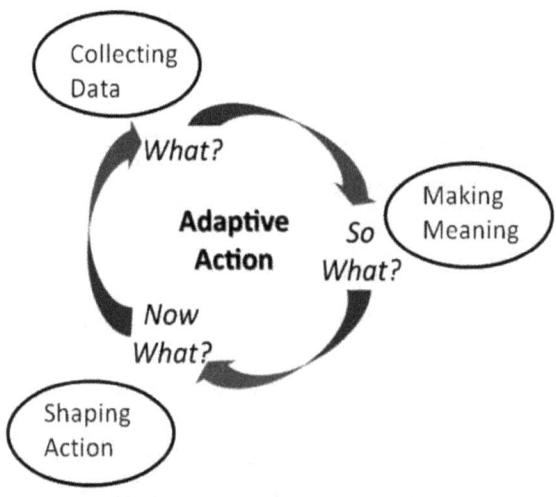

By the way, it is no coincidence that you will find Adaptive Action also cropping up frequently throughout this book. This robust tool is so intuitive, basic, and simple that it makes sense to take it out in many situations. It is not the only tool you have, but it is indeed a good one to have ready.

See if you can spot its use throughout the book as you read on.

 **Simple Things to Consider:**

- Think of an everyday situation and run through the Adaptive Action Cycle answering the three questions. When you are done, consider what would be the same or different if you had just asked yourself, *What?* and *Now What?* What difference does it make for you?

## II. PERSONAL INVENTORY

At the entrance to the Temple of Apollo at Delphi, one of the most sacred places in the ancient world is the inscription, "Know Thyself." Indeed, throughout the ages, philosophers and spiritual leaders have been saying the very same thing. You may also have heard this sound advice from those in your life who care about you and your well-being.

Knowing oneself is no easy task. For most people, it is a lifelong endeavor. However, if the time has come to pause for introspection and reflection – looking back on where you have been and looking forward to where you want to go – then you are in the right place.

Your **Personal Inventory** is a simple tool to help you start setting the conditions for change. You will begin to gain skills, knowledge, and a potential shift in perspective.

When you "know yourself," by saying it out loud and seeing it on paper in front of you, you can act with confidence and competence by yourself and with others; and anything is possible.

*On the next pages are three questions. Read them through and consider your answers. When you are ready, write down your responses.*

## ONE SIMPLE THING

1. What strengths and skills do you bring to this change effort? Hint: Modesty doesn't count. No doubt you have plenty of experience, expertise, talents, abilities, education, training, personal traits, and assets, just to get you started.

_____
_____
_____
_____
_____
_____

2. What are your growth areas, e.g. areas that could benefit from learning and development? Hint: Everyone – including you – has flaws, has faced obstacles, and has struggled with critical feedback at some point. This is a time for honesty; being aware of your growth and development areas is actually a good thing.

_____
_____
_____
_____
_____
_____

## Chapter 5. Simple Tools

3. How will you go about seeking and promoting your learning, growth, and development? Identify at least one strategy now for addressing a particular challenge. Then think about adding other strategies and ideas as you work your way through this book. Hint: Be specific, set measurable goals, and challenge yourself.

_____

_____

_____

_____

_____

_____

One Simple Thing you can do is start to pay attention to your everyday responses, habits, traits, and preferences; keep a running inventory about yourself. People often write things down so as not to forget, especially the most important things. Your learning and growth are especially important, so maybe writing it down isn't a bad idea. An enhanced level of self-awareness can be a powerful asset and opportunity.

 **Simple Things to Consider:**

- Having completed your personal inventory, what did you learn, what can you use immediately, and what concerns do you have about your responses?

### III. WORD PATTERNS

Each of us is the sum of our parts. At any given time, you may take on a particular role or responsibility, but none of us are only one thing. You are a parent, chemist, volunteer, golfer, chef, Buddhist, poet, mentor, skier, believer, cancer survivor, improvisation artist, geek, sister, etc.

The many aspects of your life are bundled together, and no matter how hard you try to keep them separate, patterns emerge, as well as interdependencies and connections. Let's see what that looks like through **Word Patterns.**

Below I have identified five facets of life, with my own particular definitions.

- *Physical:* maintaining a healthy quality of life that supports wellness and healthy habits
- *Professional:* your job, chosen career or area of expertise
- *Family:* the people closest to you, often connected by lineage and occupying a mutual living space
- *Community:* fellowship with others sharing common characteristics or interests
- *Spiritual:* peace and harmony in your life, congruent with your values and beliefs and the world

There are many variations on this idea, and you may not agree with these five in particular. You might want to substitute Culture for Community, or perhaps not include Family at all. I have selected this particular list as merely one representation of how we divide our time, energy, passion, skills, and talents, and ask you to focus on these. You may believe your family is decidedly separate from your professional life, but is that really

## Chapter 5. Simple Tools

true? Each expression of yourself is interwoven to create the whole cloth of who you are. Nonetheless, let's try to unbraid them.

Visualize your whole self and then within that entirety, identify one part or facet at a time. Picture each of these areas alone and independent. What does that look like? Take some time to reflect and see what comes to mind.

Now, imagine those separate parts of you in an ideal world, or rather YOUR ideal world. What is the story of the Physical You, the Professional You, and so on? What does that vision reveal to you about yourself? With those pictures in mind, choose three words or phrases that would describe you in that ideal world. For example, perhaps you are politically active when you think about your Community. Or maybe you appreciate being a caregiver when it comes to your Family.

Carla, the teacher we read about earlier, might respond as follows when thinking about her ideal world.

- *Physical:* Look and feel good, healthy proactive lifestyle
- *Family:* Close-knit, caring, help support their future
- *Professional:* Making a difference in students' lives
- *Community:* Volunteer, advocate, a progressive voice
- *Spiritual:* Connecting with self and others in a place of peace

**Now it's your turn. Write down your own three words or phrases here about you in your ideal world.**

*Physical Facet:*


*Family Facet:*

# ONE SIMPLE THING

*Professional Facet:*

*Community Facet:*

*Spiritual Facet:*

Now look at what you have written down and distill your ideas into one sentence for each facet, capturing the essence of your intentions. For example, based upon Carla's responses, her one sentence as a Professional might be:

*Young people are a priority to me and I want to help them learn and succeed for as long as I can.*

**Beginning below, write down one clear sentence for each facet, based upon what you want for yourself in your ideal world.**

*Physical Facet:*

*Family Facet:*

## Chapter 5. Simple Tools

*Professional Facet:*

*Community Facet:*

*Spiritual Facet:*

Perhaps in your ideal world you believe honesty and integrity are paramount in everything that you do. What does that look like for you? You steadfastly stand firm in seeking the truth in yourself and others; you tell the truth even when it may harm you; but you do not hurt others with the truth if it can possibly be avoided. People know they can rely on you, and your word is indeed your bond. That is what counts.

Or perhaps you want to dedicate your time and energy to your career and guaranteeing financial security so your family will always be provided for. What does that look like for you? You are thoughtful in your decision-making and demonstrate a strong work ethic; are industriousness and reach out to learn from others with a focus on networking and growing your business; and you are a model of diligence for others.

Or perhaps you want to take a year-long sabbatical to renew your body and mind, write a book, or reconnect with family and friends you have lost touch with over the years. What does that look like for you?

*All of these patterns will center on who you are or aspire to be, what's important to you, and how you want to connect with others.*

- So what do your lists tell you?
- What patterns do you see?
- What does it mean?
- What do you need to do?

***Brainstorm these ideas for yourself and then using the space below write down whatever thoughts pop into you head. Try not to edit what you write – just get it all down.***

Finally, look back at your words, phrases, sentences, and, of course, patterns. These represent your ideal world – and there you are front and center.

Now think about where you are right at this moment. In today's reality, what is the same and what is different from your ideal world? For example, what may be the same is your dedication to your family. What may be

## Chapter 5. Simple Tools

different are the resources you have available now for taking care of them and their future.

*Using the table below and your own previous responses, list what is the same and what is different.*

| SAME | DIFFERENT |
|---|---|
|  |  |

How large or small is the gap between today's reality and your ideal world? That may be where your path and Theory of Change start. For example, if your indicator of success is having ample financial resources and a comfortable cushion of savings for your retirement, then the patterns that would help you achieve your goal might be patterns of careful budgeting and saving, or patterns of restraint when making discretionary purchases.

This is exactly what change is about. And as you continue to understand your actions, decisions, and their relationship to who you are, your map and path will become clearer.

 **Simple Things to Consider:**

- Have you ever been told, "You are just like your father (mother, uncle, brother ... )!"? Think about that for a moment. Now select one facet of your life and your dad's (or other's), and identify three words or phrases that fit each of you in your own ideal world. Are they the same or different? What might be the underlying patterns for you both? What does that mean for you?

- Have you ever asked yourself, "How can I be so different from my brother (or sister) when we were both raised in the same house?" Next time you think that, stop and reflect. What are the similarities and differences between the two of you? How does he or she compare with you? What are the underlying patterns and what do they mean for you in your interactions and relationship today?

## IV. DIALOGUE FOR ONE

As a youngster I grew up and attended public school in New York. During recess or organized playtime I recall participating in a favorite child's game called *Do As I Say and Not As I Do*. It was a simple diversion which

## Chapter 5. Simple Tools

encouraged movement and coordination, thinking, observing, and listening. The teacher or leader would stand in front of the group and say,

- Hands on head!
- Hands on knees!
- Hands on toes!
- Hands up to the sky!

And all the while, as she was directing the group to do so, she was also putting her hands on her head, and hands on her knees as she told the children to do. Then suddenly she would say, "Hands on shoulders!" and at the same time she would reach for the sky.

Invariably a good number of us also reached for the sky, then laughed, and we were out. The last person left standing in the group became the new leader. It was always a fun game, full of giggling and groaning.

Even then we knew that our actions were meaningfully louder than our words, and that they counted – perhaps even more than what we said. So how is it that when we find ourselves in a particular situation, and we know what the best actions might be, we tell ourselves one thing, yet do something else? For example, Jim has purchased a membership at a health and fitness club, but never uses it. And Carolyn fills all her free time watching cooking shows on television or online, yet her diet often consists of ready-to-eat meals from the local supermarket's take-home case.

One aspect of this dynamic is your own experiences: what you automatically think, see, and feel in real time. The other aspect is the way you want to see yourself. When these two are in conflict, difficulties may arise. Jim really wants to be fit and healthy but his current patterns get in his way.

When you rely on yourself, you are using your many strengths and abilities to seek the answers. You are working to bridge the gap between where you are and where you want to be, trying to correct the incoherence between the two. That is what this book is about: understanding the values, motivation, goals, and commitments you make to yourself that firmly state you are taking responsibility for your own actions and accomplishments – and then acting to make them so.

**Dialogue for One** is a simple tool that outlines a process for using the wisdom of hindsight in planning for the future. How many times have you said to yourself, "Now I think of the perfect comeback to that offensive remark he made to me!"? You often know what you should have said or done in a situation that did not turn out as you had hoped – after the fact.

This simple tool takes you further. It allows you to revisit an event or series of events with a more objective eye. You ask yourself specific, targeted questions to review the data you have, understand what was going on, and then come up with a better response for the next time.

If this sounds familiar, it should: the questions are sorted by *What, So What,* and *Now What,* and present you with the opportunity to review past actions and draw out your responses in a manner that illustrates the underlying patterns that guide your behavior.

*The term **dialogue** is used here intentionally; it is more than just chatter or musings. Dialogue is a deliberate engagement between or among individuals, exploring a particular topic or problem. The exchange may be weighed by one's own views, beliefs or feelings. It goes beyond the notion of "self-talk," which is a popular expression and practice used in many self-help arenas. Dialogue is the tool you use when you want to explore more than one side of a situation.*

There are four key ideas that feed into this method, and they originate and are adapted from a number of models used for coaching corporate executives, managers, and others.

They are:

## Chapter 5. Simple Tools

- **Situation:** What was going on at that particular moment in order to create a context for what happened?

- **Behavior:** What exactly did you do? Faced with that particular set of circumstances, how did you respond?

- **Intention:** What were you setting out to accomplish? In that moment, what was your objective?

- **Impact:** As a result of the situation, your behavior, and your purpose, what was the result or effect of what actually happened?

In moving through this process, it becomes clear how you can anticipate one thing and wind up with something else. So you ask yourself how that happened and revisit your thinking and actions. Your goal is to create change for the better.

On the following page you will see a sample of this tool as if it were completed by Carla, our teacher, after an altercation with her school principal. What do you see in her responses, and what does that tell you about her?

## DIALOGUE FOR ONE

Setting the scene: Carla had an altercation with her school principal.

| WHAT | | | SO WHAT | | NOW WHAT |
|---|---|---|---|---|---|
| What Happened? (Just the facts!) | What was your intention? | What did you do exactly? | What was the impact of your actions? Are your responses helping or hurting you? | What patterns do you see? What patterns would you like to create? How can you be more effective? | What will you do differently next time? How will you work to change your patterns? |
| Dr. Gomez criticized Carla's decision to fail one of her students. | To explain to Dr. Gomez that the student deserved his grade, as supported by performance and attendance records. | Carla lost her temper and said something unprofessional to Dr. Gomez. | Carla behaved inappropriately and was unfair to Dr. Gomez. HURTING! | Having my integrity questioned is a hot-button issue! | I will listen with an open mind and be aware of all the factors involved in making a decision. |
| Carla presented documentation to support her decision. | | She demanded a face-to-face meeting with the student and his family to present her case. | This was a no-win situation, and Carla felt that her integrity was being called into question. | I'd like to be able to step back from a contentious situation and put myself in someone else's shoes. | I will maintain perspective on the situation and suggest other potential solutions and outcomes. |
| The student's parents are generous donors to the school. | | She slammed out of the office in a huff. | Carla believes students should be held accountable for their actions. | Dr. Gomez is always on my side; I have to be open to other solutions. Sometimes I need to see what is going on right in front of me. | I will understand that neither my integrity nor ability is being challenged |

Adapted by M. Tytel from Advantage Coaching and Training, Inc. © 2015 All Rights Reserved

## Chapter 5. Simple Tools

As you work your own way through this model, you will recognize that some, if not all, of this dialogue, is already going on inside your head every time you are faced with challenges, conflicts, or even simple, routine concerns. This produces a running commentary about everything you do; and seldom lets anything go by without some remark, observation, or evaluation. And once you begin to use this information more purposefully, you may be surprised by what emerges.

Think about an event or situation in the past that, in all honesty, did not go well or as expected. It may be a situation in either your personal or professional life. Such an event may be what is termed a *defining moment*, which measurably altered your course; or something that occurred in an otherwise unremarkable day, yet left a definite impression. In fact, it is also worthwhile to look at commonplace occurrences, too, to identify the less obvious, but recurring patterns that stay with us. You choose.

**With your particular event in mind, it is your turn to complete your own Dialogue for One. Answer the questions in each column of the work sheet on the next page and see what emerges.**

**Finally, complete this tool once more, except now think about a past event or situation that actually went quite well – in fact, better than anticipated. Again, answer the questions in each column of the worksheet and see what you discover.**

## DIALOGUE FOR ONE

Setting the scene:

| WHAT | | SO WHAT | | NOW WHAT |
|---|---|---|---|---|
| What Happened? (Just the facts!) | What was your intention? | What did you do exactly? | What was the impact of your actions? Are your responses helping or hurting you? | What patterns do you see? What patterns would you like to create? How can you be more effective? | What will you do differently next time? How will you work to change your patterns? |
|  |  |  |  |  |  |

## Chapter 5. Simple Tools

*Individuals often talk about **defining moments**: life-altering events, opportunities, misfortunes, milestones, critical choice points, or personal flashes of insight. As you can see, the concept of change is always implicit, though not necessarily explicit, at these times.*

*Usually defining moments happen in an instant; and are remembered long after they occur. They can be earth-shattering, such as the 2004 Indian Ocean tsunami, believed to be the deadliest tsunami in history, or personally momentous, such as the day you proposed to your boyfriend. These events may be positive and planned, e.g. college graduation or the birth of your first child, or negative and inexplicable from your perspective, e.g. an international terrorist attack or the sudden death of a loved one.*

*What do you see in your own responses?*

Your choices define these events, and these events help define you. A colleague of mine believes that defining moments help you discover your true purpose in life. Whether they result in a critical move forward or a significant stop, these simple moments define who we are, and any/every moment has the potential to be a defining moment.

So what does Dialogue for One tell you about yourself? Here are some questions you might want to ask yourself.

- Were you honest with yourself in looking back on these events?
- What were your feelings at the time and afterwards?
- Are you responses, indeed, hurting or helping you?
- What are the patterns that emerged; how were they the same and different in your two scenarios – one successful and the other less-than-successful?
- Were there any surprises?
- What did you (re)learn about yourself?

- Were these events defining moments? How do you know?

Remember, all of your patterns shape who you are. Think about your patterns of interaction, e.g. the patterns of words you use to build goodwill and better relationships with others. Think about the patterns that allow you to express what you believe, e.g. patterns of action you take, with candor and caring, and without hurting yourself or another. And think about how those patterns frame your best self – however you define that – and allow you to learn and grow.

Finally, think about how One Simple Thing, in the moment or over time, can alter a situation and lead to a completely different outcome for you and others around you.

**Simple Things to Consider:**

- Which experiences will help you learn and practice new behaviors to shift your patterns?

- What obstacles do you see before you?

- As your behavior shifts to support new patterns, what remains the same? What is different?

## V. DECISIONSCAPE

My name is Mallary and I'm a walkaholic. Each morning, Ranger – my dog, not my alarm – wakes me up at 5 a.m., and after I have taken him through his early morning ritual, I start my own. I pull on my familiar blue hoodie with the extra-large pockets and load them accordingly: cell phone,

## Chapter 5. Simple Tools

tissues, ID, and a handful of one-dollar bills. Sunglasses around my neck and reflector cap on my head, I am off on my four-mile-plus morning trek.

Just so you know, a day without a walk leaves me cantankerous and out of sorts. I need my outdoor fix every dawn to start the day. Of course there are times when it is just not possible to scratch the itch. Rational explanations, however, do not quench my craving. Like I said: walkaholic.

Once I settle into new a location, I conduct a thorough reconnaissance of the region to scope out the best options. A busy route is obviously not a good choice and can be unpredictable. Quiet, varying terrain is preferred, so I can feel both challenged and satisfied when I return. There is nothing wrong with sidewalks, though I like the feel of asphalt beneath my feet. I am out every day I can in rain, sleet, freezing temperatures, and fog; only black ice gives me pause.

Walking by far is the most popular form of physical exercise in the United States, among other places; and since many people walk somewhere, it is easy to take it for granted. Not me. Walking is not only good for my body – burning calories, staying fit, and reducing the risk of heart disease – I do some of my best thinking while walking in the hours before the sun is up. And just when you think you are in a rut, a mountain lion crosses the trail, twenty feet in front of you, looks at you once, and continues on its way. Yes, this actually happened to me.

Encouragement is easy. I am invigorated and inspired by a brilliantly changing horizon, I find peace of mind studying landscapes and cloud formations, and I maintain a positive outlook getting to know the lights in the distant skies. Walking is beyond prescribed exercise. It ignites my energy, stokes my creativity, and contributes to my peace of mind. Whatever pathology is embedded in this gnawing impulse for walking, it is good for me and it works.

Making decisions is something you do all the time, from the routine and inconsequential, to those decisions that can have a drastic impact on your life. In a complex world, decision-making can become more challenging, perplexing, and just plain nerve-wracking.

You gather information; weigh the pros and cons, including risks, rewards, and your own motivation; identify your options; and then make up your mind. Of course you can put it off with an endless search for "enough" data or delegate the responsibility to a group vote or the toss of a coin. On the other hand, decision-making – choosing between two or more courses of action – is about you and is a reflection of your patterns, and possibly the ongoing dialogue in your head. The decisions that count are the ones you make based upon who you are, what is important to you, and how you want to connect with others. This is where a **DecisionScape** comes in handy; and in my experience, I've found that decisions are fundamentally based upon *Motivation* and *Clarity*.

Psychologists define **Motivation** simply as the desire to do something. It can be the difference that makes a difference when you identify, establish, and then push onward to realize the goals you have set for yourself.

According to Dr. Jeffrey Nevid, "Motives are the 'whys' of behavior - the needs or wants that drive behavior and explain what we do." They supply the rationale for the decisions we make, though there is definitely more to it than that.

- *Motivation can be attributed to external grounds*, such as winning a prized award or receiving recognition or celebrity. You practice your golf swing in anticipation of the local club tournament and seeing the winner's trophy with your name on it.
- *Motivation can be ascribed to internal grounds,* such as the self-satisfaction of reaching a personal or professional milestone, or standing up for a cause that is aligned with your values and beliefs. You work hard to graduate with honors because you are the first person in your family to attend college.

## Chapter 5. Simple Tools

- *Motivation can be high or low* depending upon the degree of difficulty or appeal afforded by your choices and the consequences, positive or negative. Your son does his homework in order to get a passing grade for the semester. Your daughter studies for finals to boost her grade point average in order to expand her college selection options.
- *Motivation can be about the personal appeal of an activity for you.* As a customer service representative, you are constantly interacting with others. Kayaking before dawn at the lake with only the birds for company feels like heaven.
- *Motivation can center on consequences or outcomes,* which can be positive or negative. Getting up and out of the house thirty minutes earlier every day helps you beat the traffic. When an afternoon meeting runs an hour later than planned, your commuting time is doubled.
- *Motivation can be outcome-focused* and simply about the goal. You are driving across the United States, from Florida to Oregon, because you have to be in Portland. What matters is getting there.
- *Motivation can be process-focused* and about the pursuit. You are driving across the United States, from Florida to Oregon, to explore parts of the country you have only heard about and wish to see and experience for yourself. What matters is the "going."

When exploring each of these factors, it is not difficult to find similarities, differences, and, of course, evidence of your patterns. So how do you attach perspective and purpose to a particular action?

Well, it's about you. For example, you may accept the offer of a mediocre job because the mortgage is coming due and you need to take care of your family. Your pattern of taking responsibility is commendable, yet it is not the same as finding fit between yourself and your ideal job.

*That* job is the one you accept because it speaks directly to your passion, addresses the causes you care deeply about, and incidentally helps you pay the bills. *Who you are?* You pass up hard-to-get tickets to a popular music event because you have a critical deadline looming. *What's important to you?* You write and send a letter every week to your grandson living abroad; sure, technology is more efficient but he loves receiving mail and reading your stories. *How do you want to connect?*

It's entirely up to you to recognize and realize your motivation, and the simple checklist below may help. I have populated it with data from my own criteria for walking.

## WHY: YOUR MOTIVATION CHECKLIST

| | | | |
|---|---|---|---|
| **External Factors** | I can still wear a size 8 | | |
| **Internal factors** | Good health is a great gift | | |
| **Difficulty** | I am challenged by the varied terrains | | |
| **Personal appeal** | Being outside and alone in the quiet | | |
| **Consequences (+, -)** | I get to enjoy dessert whenever I want | | |
| **Outcome focused** | I can complete the course | | |
| **Process focused** | I could walk for hours on end | | |

## Chapter 5. Simple Tools

Using this example, you can see how straightforward it is to distill the "whys" and key ideas of your effort; and then fill in the information.

Now think about how you will go about accomplishing your task. This is **Clarity**: articulating *what* you will need and *how* you will go about reaching your goal.

Clarity is often expressed through sharpness, awareness, intelligibility, discovery, empowerment, and transformation. This means zooming in on the sights, sounds, and details as well as zooming out for a broader perspective on your task. For example, if you were to envision your own daily walking routine and the resources needed, you might identify the following points.

- Trail map, water, healthy snack
- Timeframe or schedule
- Hard and soft equipment
- Others involved
- Obstacles identified and ways to overcome them
- Measurement of effort
- Potential recognition for the effort

The "what" and "how" will focus on walking safely and smartly, following procedures, guidelines, and good practices, such as:

- Wearing suitable apparel to meet the current outdoor conditions, ensuring physical protection from the elements, and using insect repellent.
- Taking sensible precautions to keep yourself safe and free from injury.
- Letting someone know when and where you are going when you head out.

- Alternating or expanding routes to challenge yourself as your endurance grows.
- Maintaining regular healthy habits such as stretching, balancing, warming up, and cooling down.
- Tuning into and paying attention to what your body tells you, before, during, and after your trek.
- Preparing a contingency plan.
- Inviting others to join you if you'd like some company with you.
- Having fun along the way.

You decide what should and should not be included, how you will achieve your goal, the degree to which you will participate, and how you will measure success.

After all, when faced with choices, you base your decisions upon what you know and what it means.

*What do I know about walking, and what drives me to pursue or reject that behavior?*

*How does this speak to who I am, what is important to me, and my connection to the world?*

You want to be sure of the reasoning behind the action, the methodology, and the clarity, purpose, and precision in acting on it. The Clarity Checklist on the following page can help you, too, as you can see in my own responses noted there.

Chapter 5. Simple Tools

## WHAT AND HOW: YOUR CLARITY CHECKLIST

| Action Steps | Check the route, get a weather forecast | | |
|---|---|---|---|
| Who? (Key persons) | Myself | | |
| How? (Specifically) | Get a local map and track steps and conditions | | |
| When? (Completed by) | When I arrive, before morning | | |
| Resources needed | Rain gear, hat, map, compass | | |
| Accountable to | Myself | | |

The notion of the DecisionScape emerged from a conversation I had with a colleague many years ago when I completed my certification as an executive coach, and began working with clients. Katherine and I talked about how and why each of us reacts and behaves in various circumstances. In any situation you are called upon to make a decision and act upon it. Your behavior and choices will be based upon your own motivation and clarity, and the criteria you identify and depend on to help make your decision.

To create your DecisionScape, you start with a simple four-quadrant matrix like the one on the next page.

ONE SIMPLE THING

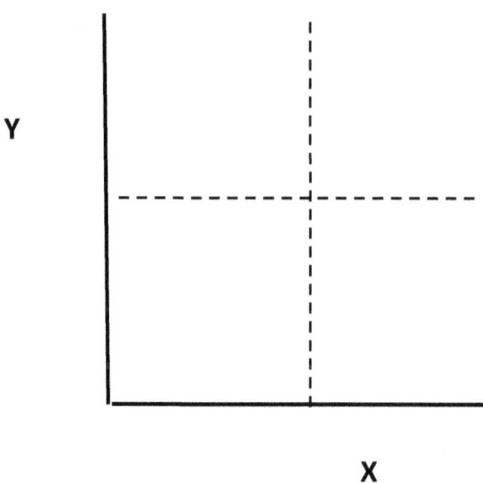

The X axis is about Motivation and allows you to plot your criteria – reasons and purpose – from low to high, e.g. the *Why* of your decision and your subsequent actions. The Y axis is about your Clarity and also plots your criteria – knowledge, awareness, and agreement – from low to high, e.g. the *What* and *How*.

I walk every day because it is good for me and I want to take care of myself. I feel exhilarated by the exercise and being out in the crisp morning air, and walking helps me start my day with purpose and a solid sense of achievement. My short-term objective is comfort, safety, and completing a route of four miles every day. My long-term goal is good health, being physically fit, and maintaining my well-being.

Therefore, based upon what I know and believe about myself, and the degree to which I have met my criteria for success, I can create my DecisionScape. As you see on the next page, my trajectory is strong, sure, and calculates as high on both the X and Y axes. In addition, my clarity and motivation – as well as my progress, outcome, and results – are specific, measurable, and realistic.

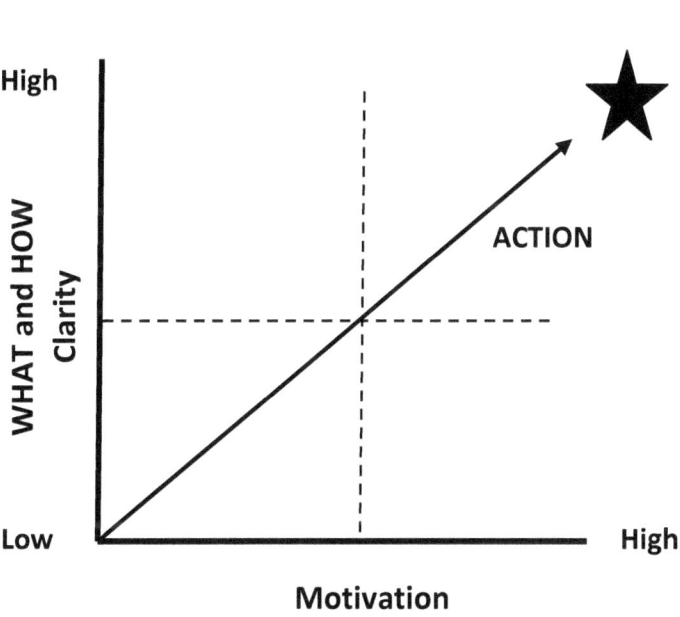

With my DecisionScape I can actually explore what I know and what it means to me, as well as keep track of my steps, landmarks, and milestones.

One surprising feature about the DecisionScape is that it tells you quite a bit about yourself, when you are truly honest in your thinking and actions.
- *Who are you*: This provides information about what you have chosen to focus on, why this is important to you, and how you will achieve it.
- *What is important to you*: You are clear this endeavor is a good fit for you, and your motivation is authentic.

# ONE SIMPLE THING

- *How do you want to connect in the world*: In this particular case, you choose to both literally and figuratively explore the pathways beyond your comfort zone, challenging your confidence and competence.

The DecisionScape is also one of my favorite tools not only because it is simple to understand and apply, but it holds you (and me!) accountable, particularly when you get carried away with yourself.

My Own Case in Point:

*As a walker and an East Coast gal, I have always felt the draw and spell of the Appalachian Trail, one of the longest continuously marked footpaths in the world. Extending almost 2,200 miles from the southern to the northern terminus, the Trail courses through fourteen states and stretches along the heights and basins of the Appalachian mountain range from Georgia to Maine. It has been estimated that almost three million people visit the Trail every year, and nearly two thousand attempt to "thru-hike," e.g. walk the entire Trail in one continuous journey.*

*I have traveled on parts of the Appalachian Trail in all of the New England states and several of the Mid-Atlantic states. And I have cross-country skied into one of the Appalachian Mountain Club huts in the While Mountains of New Hampshire in the middle of February. It has, however, always been a dream of mine to one day thru-hike the Trail. Just imagine: trekking the entire Appalachian Trail would be an experience of a lifetime.*

*It would be a testament to my strength, endurance, focus, and determination to literally take a 2,200-mile walk in the woods from start to finish. This undertaking would also reawaken in me an appreciation of the beauty and magic of nature, recognize the uncertain balance and mystery of our ecosystems, and complete a monumental physical task, solely on my innate ability and force of will. Awesome!*

## Chapter 5. Simple Tools

*Of course I would have to do extensive preparation, begin a concentrated regimen of strength training to develop my endurance, muscles, and focus; identify and collect resources and equipment; find a hiking partner or team to travel with; create a detailed plan and timeline; and ... , and ... , and ....*

Truth be told, I am highly motivated to *have done* the trip; I simply love the *idea of the adventure*; and I am especially clear on basking in the *afterglow* and *glory* as I sit and tell the best stories from the trail. In reality, however, my dream is a fantasy, and an honest assessment using the DecisionScape reflects that, as you can see below.

**DecisionScape: THRU-HIKING THE APPALACHIAN TRAIL**

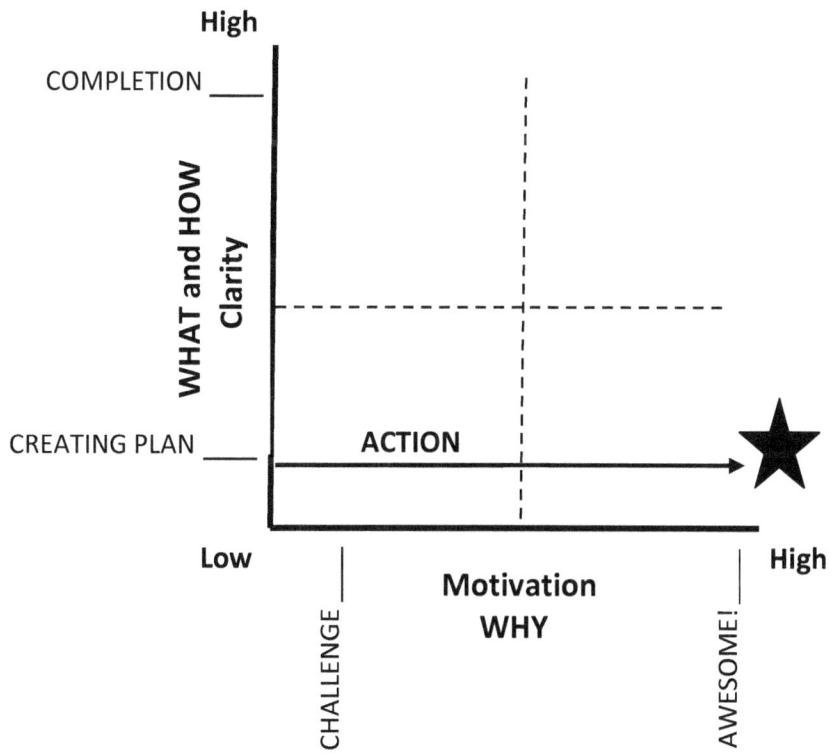

## ONE SIMPLE THING

My *motivation* is indeed high; my *clarity* – including how I am actually going to accomplish this feat – not so much.

So here is another example – Lizzie's story – of a more realistic and personal pursuit.

*Lizzie is helping her daughter, Belle, plan her wedding. Her future son-in-law, Lance, is from Madrid, and his large family will be traveling to Washington, D.C., for the ceremony and celebration. In their honor, and out of respect and affection for Lance, Lizzie has decided to learn conversational Spanish. Her motivation is obvious and authentic: she cares deeply about Belle and Lance, would like to accomplish this for herself as well as the children, and would enjoy adding Spanish to her repertoire. Therefore her secret mission is to create a warm and inviting space for both families and guests to communicate more easily, get to know each other, and build a shared familial bond.*

*Though Lizzie has long put off learning Spanish in the past, she welcomes both the task and the five-month deadline – neither to be taken lightly. She has developed a plan, and identified not only the technical resources she will need for learning at her own pace, but has also enlisted several work friends for planned and unplanned quizzing and conversation.*

*As the wedding date approaches, Lizzie knows her time will be more and more in demand, so she must carefully track her schedule and responsibilities. Her first lesson is on Tuesday and no doubt her DecisionScape will reflect success.*

After reading about Lizzie, you can probably complete her Motivation Checklist, Clarity Checklist, and DecisionScape for her, from the details in her story.

# Chapter 5. Simple Tools

*But this is about you.*

Identify an activity, venture or plan you would like to undertake. It should be something you have not quite started or fully committed to, as of yet, but are seriously considering.

Your endeavor may be personal or professional, practical or capricious, for yourself or for someone special in your life. It will be on your long-term To-Do list, and might include almost anything from an overdue home-improvement project to going back to school to completing your mystery novel to a significant life-transformation. Finally – here is an opportunity to get started on it!

**In the space below, write your objective.**

**MY OBJECTIVE:**

_____

_____

_____

Think about why you are embarking on this task.

*What are the needs, wants, purpose, and/or current circumstances that are driving your effort?*

Just as I have done, identify your own criteria. It will be based upon what **you** value and believe, allowing you to visualize your desired outcome, and quantify your achievement.

*Using Your Motivational Checklist below, list two or three Why's.*

## WHY: YOUR MOTIVATION CHECKLIST

| OBJECTIVE: | | |
|---|---|---|
| External Factors | | |
| Internal factors | | |
| Difficulty | | |
| Personal appeal | | |
| Consequences (+, -) | | |
| Outcome focused | | |
| Process focused | | |

*And WHAT will you need and HOW will you accomplish your task? Using Your Clarity Checklist on the next page, list two or three What's and How's.*

## Chapter 5. Simple Tools

## WHAT AND HOW: CLARITY CHECKLIST

| OBJECTIVE: | | |
|---|---|---|
| Action Steps | | |
| Who? (Key persons) | | |
| How? (Specifically) | | |
| When? (Completed by) | | |
| Resources needed | | |
| Accountable to | | |

- What do you see on your checklists?
- What are the emergent patterns, surprises, or gaps?
- What do they mean?

You are now ready to plot your own DecisionScape. The factors on your checklists help you set the conditions for success. Each builds upon the one prior to create a critical level of quality for your success. Analyzing and then meeting each factor helps you distinguish genuine effort and purpose from whimsy or distraction. Finding an easy path to success is unrealistic; however, your energy, enthusiasm, and commitment are what will propel you forward.

**MY DecisionScape**

**MY OBJECTIVE:**

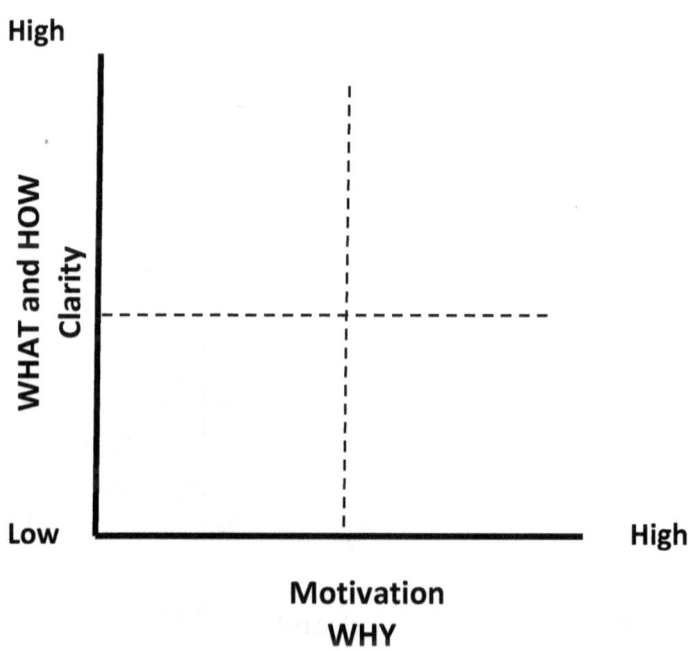

*What is the potential trajectory and accomplishment of your effort?*

# Chapter 5. Simple Tools

*Is your objective the right fit for you at this time?*

*What does this tell you about yourself and your efforts to create change?*

 **Simple Things to Consider:**

- How does a dream of accomplishment become a fantasy?

- Conversely, how does a fantasy become a genuine accomplishment for you?

- What conditions and patterns need to shift for you to reach a seemingly overwhelming goal?

- What patterns do you see in your endeavors that support and sustain your success, or get in the way of you reaching your goal?

- What are the patterns that lead you to strive for a persistent, demanding, idealistic or unlikely goal in the first place?

By the way, if the Appalachian Trail is calling out to you or you are on the lookout for an adventurous and highly human read, I absolutely recommend, *A Walk in the Woods* by Bill Bryson, about his own trek along the Appalachian Trail.

## VI. DIVERGENT ROADS

> *"Good thoughts yield good things. The future, no matter how dark it seems, can always change, as long as the thoughts change."*
> — R.A. Montgomery, 1936-2014
> Creator and founder of
> *Choose Your Own Adventure*

Have you ever read one of the popular children's books that allows you to step into a character's role and choose what happens next?

Since 1975, the *Choose Your Own Adventure* books have given millions of young people the chance to decide the fates of their heroic characters, and their thrilling outcomes. Will you journey under the sea amid creatures of the deep, or perhaps come face-to-face with the abominable snowman in the Himalayas?

In the publisher's own words, *"You and YOU ALONE are in charge of what happens in this story. There are dangers, choices, adventures, and consequences. YOU must use all of your numerous talents and much of your enormous intelligence. The wrong decision could end in disaster - even death. But, don't despair. At any time, YOU can go back and make another choice, alter the path of your story, and change its result."*

## Chapter 5. Simple Tools

Not only do you take on the role of the story's plucky protagonist, but each story allows you to select your champion's next harrowing mission, and save the day. What could be better than that?!

Well now you are an adult who can once again choose your own adventure. Think of it as approaching a significant fork in the road, just like the drawing below.

You can certainly keep right and continue in the direction you are currently heading. So far so good, right? Except that by reading this book, *you have chosen change – to plot a new course that will transport you from where you are now to where you want to be.*

So the path to the left it is; and you bring with you your experience, skills, passion, and values.

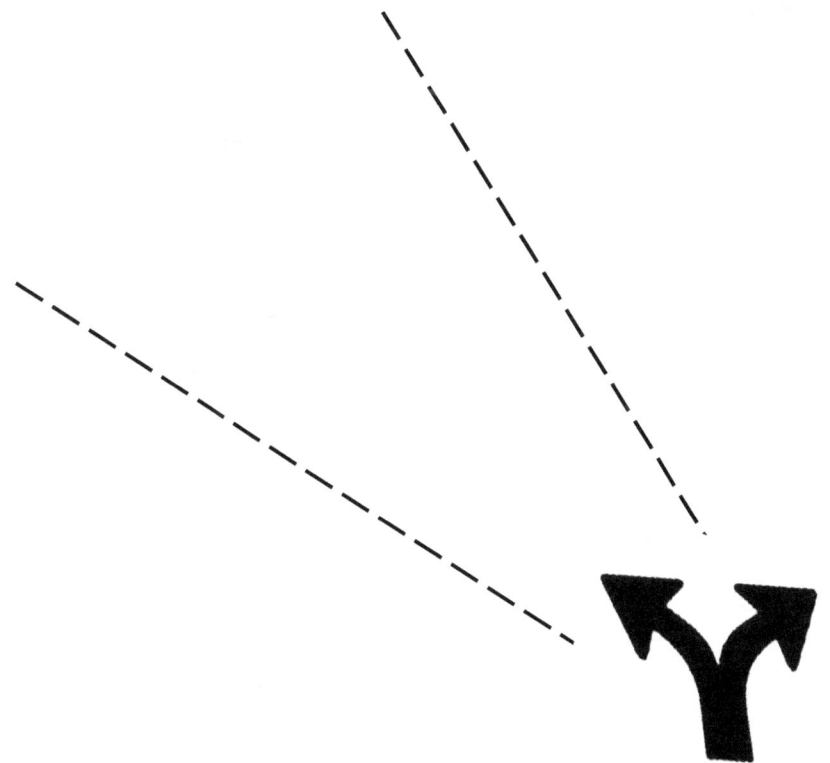

Change, however, can be very much like trying to maintain your balance and stride on three parallel but separate moving walkways. On the left is the track that has gotten you to where you are today. On the right is the track that will take you to where you want to be tomorrow. The middle track operates in a manner similar to a rail or train switch track, helping you transition from one path to another.

As you move ahead now, take some time to look back on the various decisions and choices you made getting to this point. You have much to be proud of.

**Step 1. Identify three significant accomplishments from your past and write or draw them on the road diagram above, on the left side of the road.**

Now look ahead and imagine it is some time forward in the future. Though your path is a bit unclear, you know where you are going.

**Step 2. Identify three significant accomplishments that would exemplify success in your desired future. Write or draw them on the road diagram above, on the right side of the road.**

Right now you are at a critical waypoint on your journey. Since you started reading this book, you have achieved a new depth of understanding and self-awareness, beginning with appreciating your place in the world, and your ability to influence the world.

Having reached this fork in the road, look once more at the road diagram above. Where have you been and where do you want to go? What will you do to bridge the gap between the two, to flip that switch, and move into the future? What do you know, what does it mean, and what are you going to do?

Chapter 5. Simple Tools

***Step 3. After taking time to reflect, write or draw your thoughts, questions, and hopes in the middle of the diagram above, directly on the road ahead and the path you have selected.***

Ready? It's time to get to work!

 **Simple Things to Consider:**

- "A fork in the road" is a favored metaphor for persuasion, helping someone make up their hesitant mind, or simply bringing about change. When have you come upon a fork in the road?

- What circumstances, behaviors, or patterns brought you to that decision point?

***A SIMPLE RECAP:***

*WHAT DO YOU KNOW?*

I.  You know about Complex Adaptive Systems, your ability to influence, and what that means for you.

II.  You know about Patterns – your own and those of others – and whether they are a good fit.

III.  You know about Radical Inquiry, and have begun to explore who you are, what is important, and how you want to connect with others and the world.

IV.  You know about Simple Rules, and creating a set of guidelines that help you think and act in the moment, and over time.

V.  You have learned and explored a set of Simple Tools:

    i.  Adaptive Action: shifting in response to movement around you

    ii.  Personal Inventory: recognizing your own strengths and areas of growth

    iii.  Word Patterns: similarities and differences, and your ideal world

    iv.  Dialogue for One: seeing how your behaviors and patterns are helping or harming you

    v.  DecisionScape: decision-making by understanding your true motivation and clarity about the task at hand

    vi.  Divergent Roads: transitioning into the future

*SO WHAT DOES IT MEAN?*

*AND NOW WHAT ARE YOU GOING TO DO?*

# JADAY

As a young boy in Assam, India, Jaday Payeng learned firsthand about nature and the ecosystem around him. It was 1979 and he saw major floods wash hundreds of dead snakes onto the river bank, erode the topsoil cover, and leave countless trees uprooted. Animals were left homeless or dead and the migratory flow of birds to the forests and wetlands was declining. Village elders told him this was the result of the deterioration of the forest cover and accompanying deforestation. The solution was to build new forests and homes for the animals.

Giving him a few bamboo plants, the elders asked Payeng to plant those as a start. He located a small piece of land on the River Brahmaputra and did as he was asked. Knowing what he had to do, he went back to the site and planted a few more saplings every day – for 34 years.

Today the trees are a flourishing forest covering 550 hectares of land and are home to many animals, including wild elephants, tigers, rhinos, and deer. In recognition and appreciation of Payeng's single-handed efforts, the Assam government named the forest after him. Said Assam's Chief Minister Tarun Gogoi, "Payeng is a true conservationist who is working generously on the issue, and he has shown what an ordinary person can do."

Payeng continues to plant and grow trees, creating new forests every day.

# Chapter 6. Theory of Change

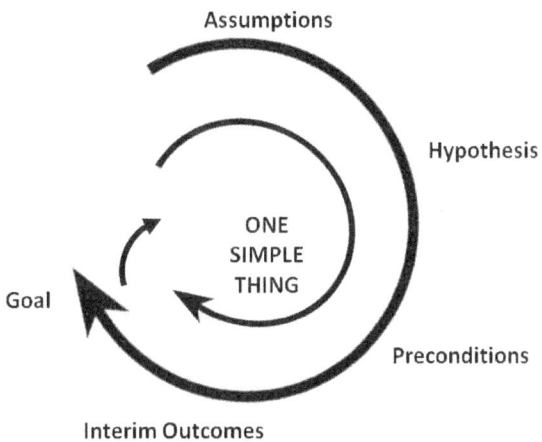

When a baby is ready to crawl, she will start by learning to balance. She will edge forward and back on arms and knees, practicing and learning as she goes. At the same time she begins to develop those muscles that will help her walk. She wants to explore her world. The more she sees, the more she wants to investigate and discover. She may choose to "bottom shuffle," but the goal is the same: getting around in her world, propelling herself forward, outward.

Next will come walking, and you will see her pulling herself up on everything within reach: tables and chairs, dogs, even Grandpa. As those muscles strengthen and her balance builds, she will learn to navigate through her own space, efficiently and independently. Before you know it and perhaps even like it, she will be running, leaping, and trying out for the varsity lacrosse team.

Crawling develops and strengthens motor skills, which leads to walking, which builds balance and extension, which leads to running, which extends and enhances stride and biomechanics. So what is it about crawling that makes it possible for children to leap and bound?

Simply put, it is a sequence of early and intermediate accomplishments that set the stage for producing long-range results. This includes a set of assumptions about the process, and identifies how these early and intermediate steps and outcomes relate to achieving long-term outcomes, and yielding an impact.

Change, like learning to walk, is a process: that means to achieve a particular goal or state of affairs; you need to engage in a series of actions, steps, or behaviors which propel you forward. You frequently know the starting point, and where you wish to finish. Sometimes, however, you are not quite clear on how the actions or pieces in between will unfold, how they are related, or if they will be successful. If you can plan and then chart this process, you can identify a set of factors involved in creating change. This will help you determine whether you have, indeed, achieved the outcomes you desire.

Individual change has a great deal to do with who you are, patterns of thought and behavior, the gaps between what is and what could be, your motivation, choices, consequences, and clarity. There are myriad options in front of you, and consequences are not always bad. Perhaps good enough really is good enough. So how do you choose?

Well, you have to decide for yourself what you want and that you want things to be different. Whatever path and destination you are aiming for, you have to step into that decision with self-assurance and take responsibility for it. Effective strategies for change must be built upon concern,

## Chapter 6. Theory of Change

care, and consideration of what you have to do. Creating personal change is sometimes tough work. With drive, purpose, commitment, and a great sense of direction the job will get done. That is where your Theory of Change comes in.

*A **Theory of Change** is a road map for creating and implementing a plan for your desired change, and includes indicators or measures of progress and accomplishment. It is designed for understanding how an individual or group expects to achieve a long-term goal. By creating and following a "causal framework," a theory of change illustrates the relationships between actions taken and how these actions or interventions lead to particular outcomes. This framework also allows you to test hypotheses and assumptions about how to best reach your goal. It is One Simple Thing after another - free of complications or distractions - that paves your way.*

The Theory of Change concept first emerged from community development initiatives in the mid-1980s to the 1990s, and the collective efforts of practitioners and evaluators to help clarify social change processes. Stakeholders involved with complex programs operating in complex systems are often unclear about how the change process will unfold. They may therefore miss the connection between the early and mid-term milestones, and the longer-term desired outcomes. Without recognizing and paying attention to this correlation, important factors could be missed entirely.

As part of this work at the time at the Aspen Institute, Carol Weiss identified the term "theory of change" to distinguish the path from initial assumptions, to specific short-term steps and activities, to short-term outcomes along the way, to the final results. According to their premise, if you could be specific about the theory of change driving your efforts as a whole, and the interim steps, you could strengthen and improve your ultimate outcome.

- Where are you now?
- Where do you want to be in the future?
- What are you going to do to get there?

Your Theory of Change begins with an unambiguous statement of your goal. For example:

*I want to run a marathon before my 40th birthday.*

In order to make that happen you have to create a reasonable hypothesis, based upon what you know and can discover about the topic; be able to measure your actions; and recognize the factors that are present and relevant.

*The **hypothesis** is the encapsulation of your Theory of Change. At the highest level, your hypothesis is the steps and activities you think will be necessary to reach your goal. Through an analysis, appraisal or interpretation of a situation, you may identify and test specific actions and their resulting consequences.*

With your goal in mind, here is an example of a hypothesis consistent with your desired outcome and beliefs.

*If I can prepare myself through an ongoing disciplined regimen of diet and exercise, maintain my focus and rigor in my methods, and improve my breathing and overall stamina, then I will be able to run and complete a marathon before I am 40.*

You have now clearly stated your goal and your hypothesis. Review them and if the goal and hypothesis fit, it is time to identify your underlying assumptions.

## Chapter 6. Theory of Change

**Assumptions** are the values, beliefs, and underpinnings that help you create a context for your change effort. Assumptions need to be valid, relevant, and consistent with your goal; in other words, they need to make sense.

By asserting your assumptions, you are ensuring coherence and fit in your thinking and behaviors. Checking your assumptions may also reveal some larger theory or principle operating in the same space and time. For example, one assumption might be:

*Seeing any difficult endeavor through from start to finish strengthens one's spirit, self-assurance, and the ability to effectively contribute to the world at large.*

This assumption is clearly applicable and fundamental to your primary goal. It also embodies a much broader supposition about who you are, what is important to you, and how you want to connect with others and the world. This one stated assumption can be both a philosophy for living your life and an abiding principle for facing tough situations wherever you may find them. Assumptions create the basis for everything that follows.

Next, consider the necessary circumstances, must-haves, or Preconditions that need to exist.

**Preconditions** are specifically the pre-cursors or requirements that must be present or achieved in order for you to move on to the next step. In other words, preconditions are those short-range steps or activities put into place and accomplished along the way, and their related outcomes.

For example, preconditions for your training may include:

- You are physically active right now.
- You are in shape to reasonably take on this laborious enterprise without damaging your system.

- You have talked to your medical doctor to ensure there are no hidden disorders that would prevent you from competing or be physically dangerous to your health and well-being.
- You have enlisted a cadre of friends and family to support you in this endeavor.

If the relevant, logical criteria or preconditions are not present, you need to identify appropriate measures, actions, or interventions to help you meet them. And preconditions should not be thought of as obstacles. Instead, they should be viewed and purposefully identified to create the best possible conditions for you to succeed. They, too, are part of the building blocks of your effort and results.

Now it's time to identify the steps and tasks, including a feasible timeline that will help get you to the big day – starting now. These may include the following:

- Engaging the best fitness coach for you.
- Finding supportive training partners.
- Outlining a suitable running course and schedule.

Each action is an important step along your way, providing you with data and outcomes, and then leading to your next steps. How will you know if you've been successful? You will identify results or indicators along the way to help you assess your efforts.

**Indicators** are those factors that will help you recognize and gauge if you have been successful in reaching your targets. Indicators address and answer the following questions: who or what will be changed or achieved; when will the change happen; and how much change needs to take place for you to say, Yes, I am successful.

## Chapter 6. Theory of Change

Your indicators provide a continuous reality check with ongoing feedback – from your preconditions to your interim outcomes to your final goal. By identifying results along the way, you will ensure once again that your Theory of Change not only makes sense, but *makes sense for you.*

Indicators in support of your marathon training may focus on:

- Sharpened focus and concentration during workouts.
- Increased endurance in running time and distance.
- Honed reflexes and responses to unpredictable weather or terrain.
- Greater confidence in your own ability.

The ultimate indicator, of course, will be you crossing the finish line with scores of others, and glowing with the joy of your achievement.

A Theory of Change is often explained using a diagram that illustrates the overall framework, design, and flow of activities. These diagrams can be as detailed as you want, and should be open to revisions and updates.

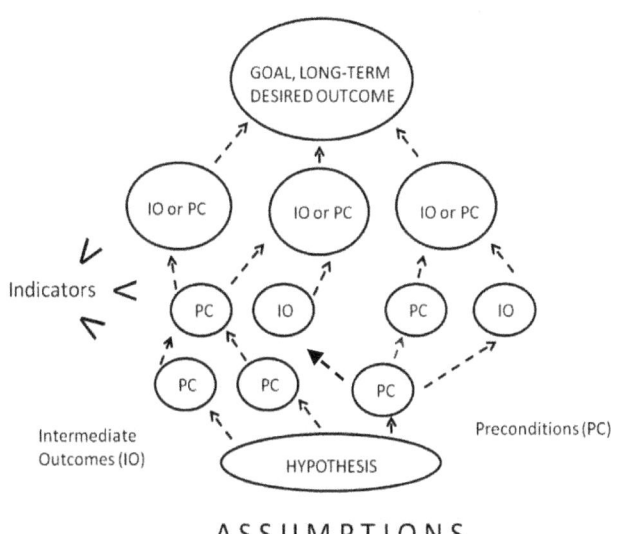

## ONE SIMPLE THING

The example shown on the previous page is adapted from *The Community Builder's Approach to Theory of Change* by Andrea Anderson, Ph.D.

As you can see, it is quite simple. Your goal at the top is large and clear, and based upon your underlying assumptions. These assumptions in turn support your hypothesis, and the actions that follow.

Moving from the bottom up, you can see your path.

- Clearly stating your assumptions.
- Understanding and naming your preconditions and interim outcomes.
- Recognizing what must be achieved to advance.
- Appreciating how the success of one step leads to next steps, and that early outcomes lead to subsequent outcomes.
- Identifying clear indicators to track and assess your efforts along the way.

Now that you have completed your first marathon, here is a different example to consider. As a parent, math teacher, principal, school board member, or anyone concerned with the well-being of your community, the following goal may be of critical importance to you.

*Every high school student in my community will stay in school and earn their diploma.*

To some people this might seem a highly unrealistic goal. Perhaps, but let's explore what it will take to get you there. Create a hypothesis that states if you complete a series of actions, then you will get the desired outcome(s) that support the achievement of your goal.

The following might be your hypothesis:

# Chapter 6. Theory of Change

*If our educators, health, and social service providers, neighborhoods, and families create sustainable patterns of protective factors that focus on programs, strategies, and relationships critical to supporting the educational success of our most vulnerable student populations, then our children will develop the confidence, motivation, support systems, and resiliency to stay in high school and graduate.*

In other words, by working together with your community, you can all support your young people to get their education, thereby increasing their opportunities and resilience for the future.

Next state your assumptions, which may be the following.

- High school students at risk can achieve academic success with an available support system.
- Connection to a community is a protective factor for developing and maintaining resiliency in teens.
- The presence of a caring adult can make a difference in the life of an adolescent.

So what will it take to get there? Your answers will be more and more specific, and include preconditions, actions, outcomes, and indicators of success.

Possible preconditions for your theory might be:

- Caring parents and family members who want to see their youngsters succeed.
- A proactive school board.
- Teachers committed to success for all their students.

From this, a potential action step and outcome might be:

- Develop a volunteer school mentoring program.
- Engage a cadre of volunteers to energize local community members and stakeholders.

And your indicators of success might be:

- The school board has allocated additional funds for a pilot mentoring program to be launched next semester.
- A project team has formed and work is underway.

How will you make that happen? Begin to list what you know, what you will need to do, and then what actions you may take, such as the following.

- Identity and/or develop a model program for your mentoring target group.
- Find and meet with potential program partners and stakeholders.
- Recruit, screen, and orient mentors.
- Communicate with young people and engage them in launching the program.
- Select students and begin to pair them with adults.
- Develop a list of program activities and resources.

Then what will you need to accomplish each of these actions? Well, you get the idea.

As you unbraid each step, the map for your Theory of Change fills with information, strategies, tactics, and outcomes. Your path becomes clearer – and don't forget that path is multi-dimensional. Every action can lead to diverse and varying outcomes in your open, nonlinear, and high dimension systems. Acknowledge, appreciate, and make the most of them.

# Chapter 6. Theory of Change

Your Theory of Change is your own; however, it can also be a shared and charted course for yourself, your community, and others who support the same or complementary goals. All along the way, be sure to recognize and take advantage of individuals and resources around you that can provide support, and help you meet your goal.

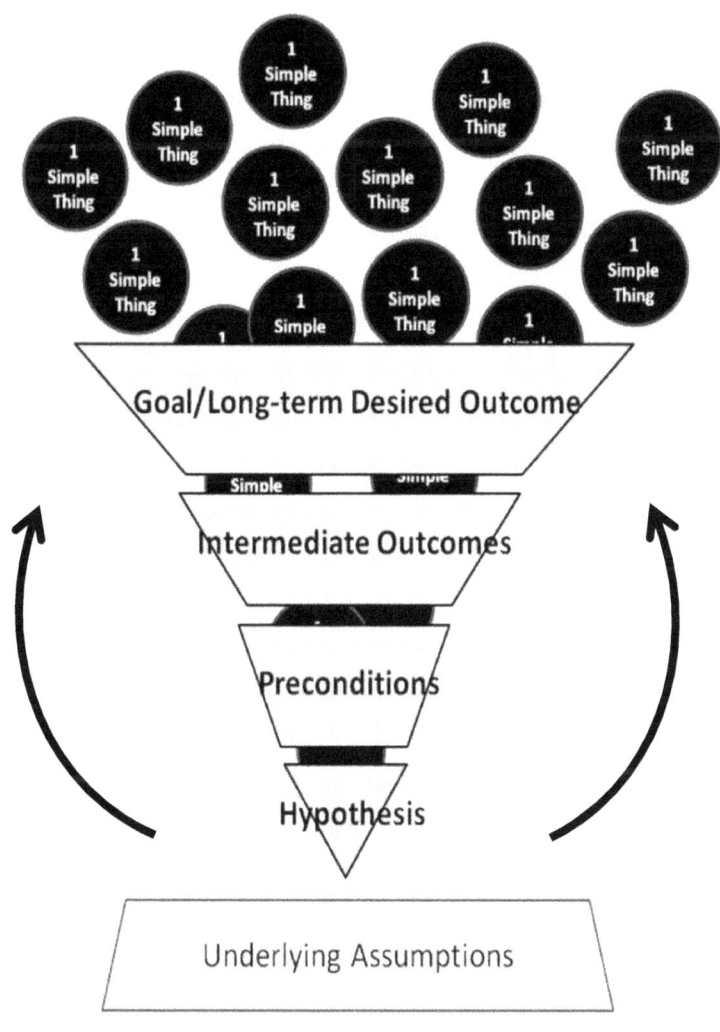

 **Simple Things to Consider:**

- Creating your Theory of Change is a straightforward, values-based process, through which you can visualize and build a solid plan for action. Recognize the significance of operating in complex adaptive systems; and remember that simple is not the same as easy.

- What is the difference between *Simple* and *Easy*?

## ED

*Ed is 64 years old and has a history of chronic illness: diabetes, high blood pressure, and coronary heart disease. Twelve years ago he had quadruple bypass surgery. Through the miracles of modern medicine and a brilliant, committed team of caregivers, he continues to do well. He maintains his health through a range of medications, and though he is aware of the importance of regular exercise and a healthy, controlled diet, he will not think twice about having pizza or dessert. Since a foot injury last summer, his regular exercise routine has become extinct.*

*His doctors consistently recommend making changes; their Theory of Change for Ed is defining clear, reasonable goals, resources, and activities that are within Ed's capability and reach. This includes improved eating habits, regular moderate exercise, and working with a personal health coach to get his weight and blood pressure better under control. Ed has seen a nutritionist and listened carefully to her assessment and recommendations. It definitely made sense, and Ed's wife is supportive and energetic in her efforts to provide what Ed needs. She also urges Ed to start riding his bike again. That is something they can do together, since he is not interested in joining her when she goes to the gym.*

*The thing is, Ed is content to let his medications do the work for him. It is not that he does not care; he is just not interested in changing. What Ed is doing seems to be working fine for him. His way of thinking (and his hypothesis for change) is this:*

## ONE SIMPLE THING

*If I continue to monitor my condition, remain diligent in my prescription regimen, and see my doctors regularly, then I can continue to maintain a quality of life that allows me to get from one day to the next with relatively little discomfort.*

*An indicator of success for Ed is a good number for his sugar level when his regular blood work returns from the lab.*

*Ah! This is an excellent example of a Theory of Maintenance, but it is not a Theory of Change!*

## Chapter 7. Simply Acting with Intention

**YOUR GOAL**

A Theory of Change articulates how one thing leads to another; and in order to create change, you must believe in the change process, and that it will work. In this case, that means a planned sequence of events forms the foundation for what is ahead.

Actions are connected to outcomes; outcomes are connected to each other; and success can be measured all along your path. It is up to you to create your story and decide why your Theory of Change makes sense for you. It is YOU that sets the conditions for change.

The context is created by underlying assumptions and the adaptive orchestration of all the moving parts. This may sound complicated, but it's not. It's the organization and coordination of One Simple Thing after another, to move you forward within your own complex environment.

The first and most important piece in this process is your goal. Throughout this book, you have been learning about yourself. You have had time to think about where you want to be, and the changes you want to create. Also, do not forget about critical connections, dependencies, and the very dynamical nature of your world.

*In the space below write your Goal or Desired Outcome*

And in the long term, how will you know if you have achieved your goal?

*In the space below, write down two or more indicators of success, keeping in mind what will be changed; when will the change happen; and the level of change that must take place for you to unequivocally say, Yes, I have reached my goal.*

→

→

→

→

**YOUR HYPOTHESIS**

*If..., then...*

In my own research and practice, I have seen that playing with various scenarios and options can build not only flexibility but vision and capacity, too. The more clearly you can see, articulate, and communicate your aspirations, and the reasons behind what you want to achieve, become, and create, the more likely you are to reach your goals. So let's begin.

## Chapter 7. Simply Acting with Intention

*If ..., then....*

Below are a number of sentence starters for you. Try them on and see what you think. Do any resonate with you? How would you complete these sentences?

**As you read through them, write down whatever ideas occur to you.**

- If I see myself as part of something important and larger than just myself, then ...

- If I hold up a mirror to reflective thinking, then ...

- If I understand myself in relation to others, then ...

- If I can recognize and understand the patterns I create and hold, then ...

- If I build my own individual capacity and resiliency, then ...

- If I want to understand where I am and what my roles are within the system, then ...

- If I understand and appreciate my role and what I can contribute, then I can work collectively with others to create ...

- If I am very clear about who I am, then I can construct productive partnerships and communities to ...

- If I can influence and create a bridge connecting what I have now and what I want, then I can ...

As you are thinking and scribbling, you are also implicitly asking yourself the following critical questions.

- Why am I continuing to pursue my current path if it does not fit?
- What have I learned about myself?
- What will it take for me to engage in this process?
- What will participating in this process help me achieve, or make possible for me?
- What is it going to take to transform myself?
- What will it take for me to get to that point?
- When is the right time to act?
- *What will it take to identify and create the patterns I want to sustain; to influence and shift to the most healthy, productive and sustainable patterns for myself?*

Don't forget that at its highest level, your hypothesis will articulate what steps and activities you think are necessary for you to reach your goal. Your answers lie in what you truly know about yourself.

**My overarching hypothesis for this work is simply this:**

*If I can access a set of simple tools to see and understand my patterns and how they are helping or harming me, understand who I am, what is important, and how I want to connect with others in the world, and create a basic framework to guide my patterns of thought, behavior, and decision-making,* **then** *I can identify and accomplish One Simple Thing every day to reach my goal and realize a productive, sustainable, and fit life.*

## Chapter 7. Simply Acting with Intention

You have identified your goal; now you need to state your own hypothesis. Based upon what you have learned, and your own critical questions, what action will you take? How will you frame your own Theory of Change?

**In the space below, write your hypothesis.**

**If ...**

**Then ...**

Supporting your hypothesis – and ultimately your actions – are your underlying assumptions, those truths you hold and believe in, with or without empirical evidence.

**The following are the assumptions I have used in creating this work and writing this book. They are personal and explicit.**

- We are complex and adaptive individuals, and operate in complex, adaptive, highly diverse, and unpredictable systems.

- Though boundaries exist between and among us, we are all part of everything else.

- The things that are important are both personal and universal.

# ONE SIMPLE THING

- *We appreciate the differences that make a difference.*

- *We interact with others according to an individual set of principles or rules that create a framework for all else.*

- *Each of us seeks to build capacity and resilience, as we ourselves define those qualities.*

- *We strive to create a healthy, productive, and sustainable life according to who we are, what is important, and how we want to connect in the world.*

My assumptions have emerged from learning and practice, reflection and growth, and resolutely occupying a space of inquiry. Your own assumptions must offer meaning and purpose to you.

**Using the space below, identify one or more of the assumptions underlying your change effort.**

→

→

→

→

Chapter 7. Simply Acting with Intention

Do your assumptions reflect what is true and useful for you? Do they make sense and provide a solid, enduring foundation for your efforts? You must answer that for yourself.

Now focus on your preconditions, the requirements or circumstances that should be present to support your change efforts, and reaching your goal. Think back to the example of the marathon. A precondition there was undergoing a physician's examination and getting her thumbs-up before embarking on a rigorous marathon-training regimen. Scan your environment; what do you need and what do you see around you that will buttress and sustain your own endeavors?

***In the space below, identify one or more requisites or preconditions for your change effort.***

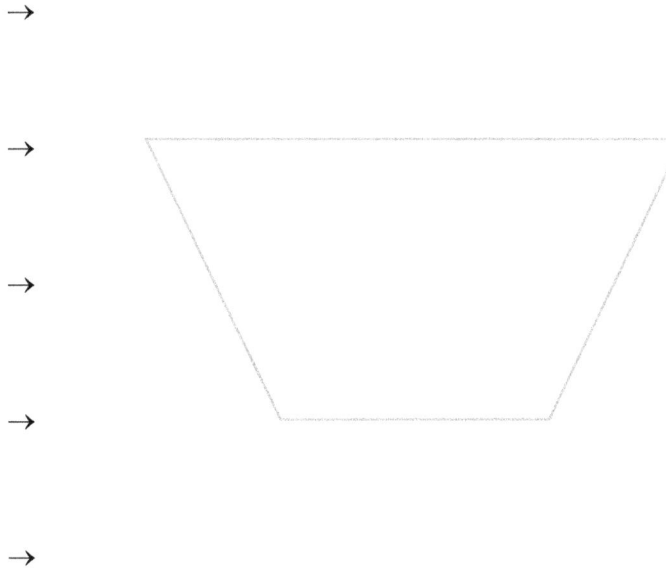

→

→

→

→

→

*And your indicators are:*

→

→

→

→

As your path emerges, it is time to act: what actions and intermediate outcomes will move you forward?

*In the space below, identify one or more steps you will take, and milestones you will reach on your way toward your goal.*

→

→

→

→

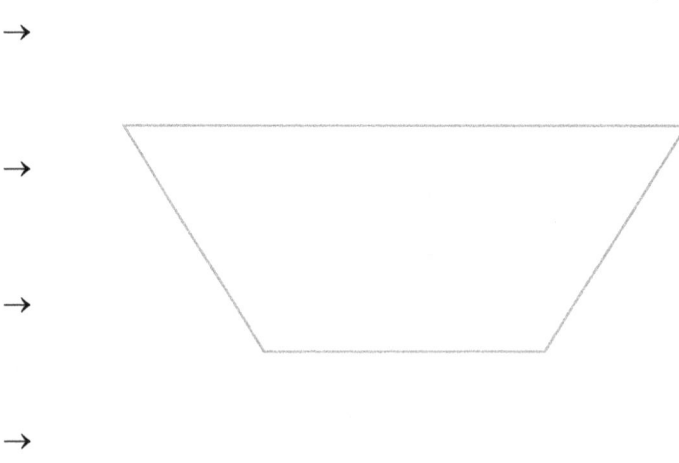

Chapter 7. Simply Acting with Intention

***And your indicators are:***

→

→

→

→

Your map is almost complete.

***Using the wealth of data you have gathered since starting this book, the self-awareness you have gained about yourself – and your deep resolve for change – add your reflections and complete your own Theory of Change diagram on the next pages.***

***Then ask yourself the following:***

- Is it credible?
- Is it doable?
- Will you be able to measure and maintain your continued success?

*Doing One Simple Thing every day is the answer.*

*INSIGHTS, IDEAS, AND NOTES TO YOURSELF ...*

Chapter 7. Simply Acting with Intention

**YOUR THEORY OF CHANGE**

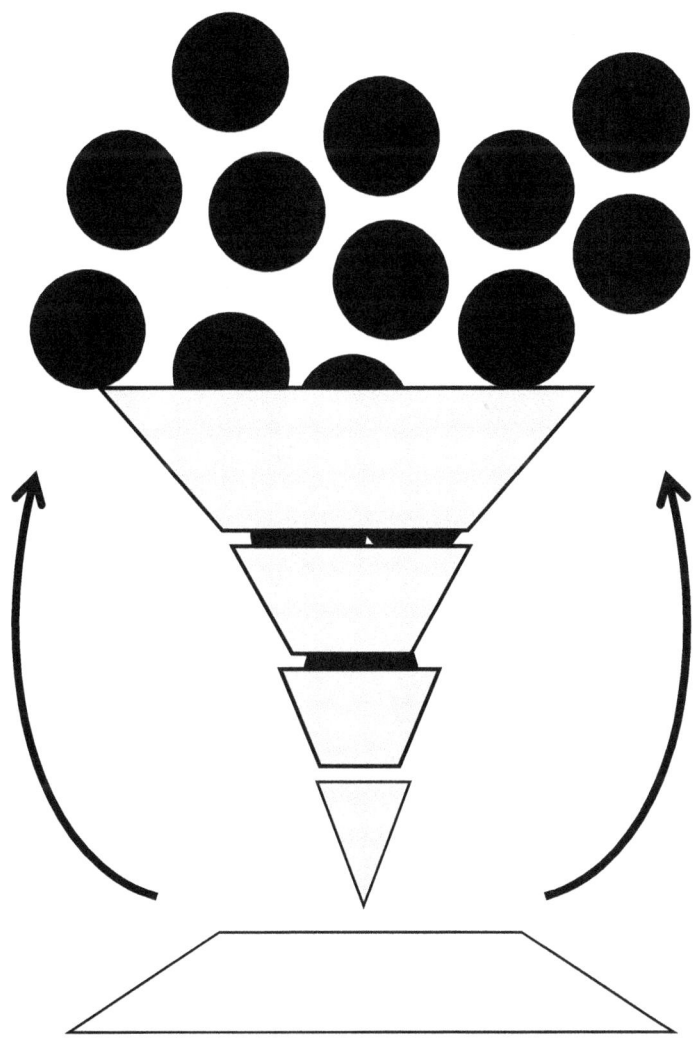

 **Simple Things to Consider:**

- You read about Ed earlier in this chapter. If Ed were someone you knew and cared about, what would you say to him?

- When can a Theory of Maintenance be the best solution in a difficult situation?

- Your Theory of Change is a personal framework for being *your best self*. How will you go about enlisting others to help you on your journey?

## IDA

Anyone who met Ida agreed she was special. A peasant, born in Ottynia, Poland, in 1864, she remained totally illiterate her entire life, never learning to read or write. Her mother died when she was quite young, leaving Ida to care for her three small brothers. Ida's father did not like to be without a wife so he soon married again and began another family with his second bride. He chose to quietly forget his first family, so Ida and the boys were left to fend for themselves.

Ida grew up and married as expected; she had two children. Her husband, typical of the time, left the family to go to America. He said when he found work he'd send for her. Instead, he divorced her and remarried once he got settled in New York.

Max had grown up fancying Ida, but when she married, he had lost his chance. Now that Ida was free, he married her, took in her two children, and they all went to America together. There, they had three additional children and settled in a welcoming neighborhood where their extended family already lived. The couple worked hard and managed, though Ida frequently said without regret or rancor that they never had more than two nickels to rub together. Not a week went by without the entire family gathering at Ida's.

## ONE SIMPLE THING

*Without knowing it, Ida set the example for generations to come. Rather than hurt another's feelings, she would willingly do without or make her own excuses. Instead of being angry or holding a grudge, she chose to go out of her way to dismiss or overlook any unkindness toward her, though she always acted quickly and with intention when standing up for others. Ida knew who she was, valued family above all else, and knew what was truly important in her world.*

*Pearl was Ida's favorite granddaughter and one of Pearl's favorite memories was of her and her grandmother standing together watching Charles Lindbergh motorcade through New York. On that day, waving with the crowds, Ida whispered firmly in Pearl's ear, "Look, my girl, at the world changing. The sky is no longer the limit. Maybe you cannot choose your life, but you can choose what to do with it. Make a good choice; make it your choice."*

# Chapter 7. Simply Acting with Intention

If you've ever embarked on a significant home renovation or considered building a new house, then you know it is not for the faint-hearted. It takes skills, patience, expertise, commitment, follow through, resources, and a plan. Blueprints are drawn by an architect or engineer and thoughtfully reflect what the homeowner desires. They show the builder exactly what to build, how to sequence and coordinate work flow, and even when the project is done. There are many tasks to manage, details to track and complete, and a series of simple organized steps to accomplish.

Your Theory of Change is your blueprint: with it you will get from where you are now to where you want to be. If it is realistic, sound, and thorough, you can work to achieve your goal, and demonstrate your learning, growth, and success. More importantly, you can also proactively and intentionally create change and achieve the outcome you want.

*Right about now you may be feeling extremely pleased about all you have accomplished – and at the same time overwhelmed. You've started with a goal and worked your way through a progression of steps, producing a huge amount of data. You have identified and explored your patterns, what drives you and why, and gained an understanding and keen awareness about yourself, one that you might not have had before. You've learned about and created a Theory of Change for yourself that will guide your next steps. You have a clear, fixed goal. And yet, you may be sitting there overcome by the extent of the work that still lies ahead.* **Now what do I do?!**

The challenge now is this: knowing what you are able to do about your behaviors, patterns, priorities, and commitments, can you seriously carry out the things that need to be done, and feel motivated and energized about making the necessary leap?

Actually, all you have to do is One Simple Thing. The pathway to change lies in intentionally living by your own values and beliefs. It starts with the simple things you can do one at a time over time, to make a difference, and get to where you want to be. You have the necessary information and structure; now start to build upon that foundation. Once the framing of the house is complete, it is time to begin installing the plumbing, wiring, and insulation. Soon you will be moving in and hanging art on the walls.

*Ralph Waldo Emerson said, "The creation of a thousand forests is in one acorn." That is the marvel and magic of One Simple Thing. Or imagine the silent, fragile beauty of a single snowflake; and yet "When they stick together," as Vesta Kelly stated, "look what they can do." That same notion applies to your work to create change.*

## Chapter 7. Simply Acting with Intention

Remember the simple pencil-and-paper game of connecting the dots you played as a child? You draw a line from one point to another, and another, and when all the dots are joined a complete picture emerges. The same is true when you begin to construct a 1,000 piece jigsaw puzzle. Each piece is an important, relevant part of the whole image, getting you to its completion, whether it's an edge, a bit of sky, or the puppy's tail.

Let's suppose you oversee the customer experience management function at your company. One of your desired patterns for service quality might be an environment of trust and rapport in your relationships. If a member of your service team knows she must be honest and open in her interactions with customers, as well as fellow employees, she can make informed, consistent, and fair choices about staff development and training. She can also respond to customers' questions and needs in creative and respectful ways; and provide helpful and productive feedback to members of her team. In other words, she can **amp** the patterns that are working and matter.

Implementing each of these actions – One Simple Thing at a time – can be as simple as being patient and kind during a call with an irritable customer; letting the team know she appreciates them at any moment of the day, as well as when they do a good job; and promptly following up on information queries, even if she has to say, "I am still working on that and will get back to you by the end of today." Each of these simple actions contributes to and supports fitness, her values and beliefs, her Simple Rules, and her desired patterns. By the way, all of the above are also productive, positive, sustainable, and good for business.

The process is exactly the same for you. All it takes is One Simple Thing to move you forward. For example, if you are seeking to **amp** your patterns of courage and spirit, there are many definitive actions you can engage in: speak out in protest of unfair laws or policies; stand up and advocate for a particular issue you believe in; report an incident you witnessed of workplace bullying. All of these are brave and worthy acts. Think of the many other simple things you can do as well: offer to help someone who seems lost. You may find you are both rewarded by that simple generous act. Or, let go of one thing that has been holding you back. Yes, go on and be daring: **damp**, and see what happens.

Acting with courage may also mean developing your own independence and sense of purpose in large and small ways: taking the stairs when everyone else is moving toward the elevator; passing on that last piece of birthday cake for someone at work you do not even know; sitting down and writing that note of apology you have been putting off.

Based upon what you now know about yourself, your patterns, and how you want to be in the world, each action is just One Simple Thing that could make a difference; so pay attention.

And that is exactly what I'd like to you to do: pay attention and watch what happens. No matter how well any project, task, or assignment is done, it is always a good idea to take some time, once completed, to conduct a straightforward "action review." This is a practice I learned while working with the U.S. Army. As the name suggests, this simple process is an opportunity for everyone – individuals or groups, rank and file – to look back on your work or behaviors, appraise and track what you have done, and apply those lessons learned in the future. Your "after" action review consists of these simple questions:

- *What worked?* Think about the situation and the actions you took. How did it go? What went well that you are proud of, pleased with, and has added value to your learning, growth, and reaching your goal? And if you know why things went well, e.g. the timing could not have been better, note that, too.

- *What didn't work?* Looking back, what did not go well, did not happen as anticipated, or did not add value to the situation and your learning? Why not?

## Chapter 7. Simply Acting with Intention

- *What changed?* When you 'Think Systems' you're attuned to see even the smallest shifts. What do they mean in this particular context?

- *What did I learn?* This question leads you right back to your patterns, and advancing you toward your desired goal.

- *What will I do differently next time?* Here is the culmination of your effort and learning. This is *your* moment of change.

Record your responses any way that makes sense to you; or you can use the One Simple Thing Worksheet at the end of this chapter. Capture your notes, highlights, insights, and reflections.

Once you have a collection of action reviews, it will be helpful to go back and revisit these worksheets over time. You may be surprised at the shifting and emergent patterns, particularly as you gain confidence in your own process of learning and development. These worksheets can be used immediately and repeatedly to reflect on current circumstances and potential opportunities. Also, they increase options for action by helping you think differently and more deeply about the ways in which you influence and are influenced by the world.

Now think back to what you have learned about yourself while reading this book. Review your patterns and behaviors, decision-making process, strengths, growth areas, and, of course, your goal.

What is One Simple Thing you can do to support any step along the way in your Theory of Change? Start with one small and simple idea, linking a particular action to a particular event. For example, here is One Simple Thing to consider.

*Instead of gnawing on what could have been, e.g. that missed opportunity to stand up and support your colleague, take a step forward and do something about it right now.*

## ONE SIMPLE THING

What does that look like and what simple action can you take for yourself as well as another, to make things right? Don't forget that the slightest pebble creates an ongoing current of ripples in a pond.

*Starting here, write down some ideas to begin your own list of simple things. Let's see what you can come up with.*

→

→

→

→

→

As your own patterns change, you are influencing and shifting patterns around you, too. Yes, with each simple thing you do, you are changing the world.

## Chapter 7. Simply Acting with Intention

| ONE SIIMPLE THING WORKSHEET |
|---|

**Date:**

**Goal:**

**My One Simple Thing:**

| WHAT WORKED? | WHAT DIDN'T WORK? |
|---|---|
|  |  |

**WHAT CHANGED?**

**WHAT DID I LEARN?**

**WHAT WILL I DO DIFFERENTLY NEXT TIME?**

# ONE SIMPLE THING

 **Simple Things to Consider:**

- What is one example you can recall from your own life when one small action created a large ripple?

- What is One Simple Thing someone in your life would appreciate you doing for them right now?

# FRANK

Frank Wills was a security guard for high-end apartments and office buildings in Washington, D.C. On June 17, 1972, he noticed something odd while doing his rounds. Pieces of tape had been placed on the latches of several doors between the basement stairwells and the parking garage of one particular building, to prevent the doors from locking. Wills removed the tape thinking it must have been left by the cleaning crew. However, when he returned on his rounds later, he found that the tape he had removed had been replaced. Realizing that something was wrong, he called the D.C. police.

The police arrived quietly, in plain clothes and an unmarked car, and were able to get past a planted lookout. Within minutes, they arrested five intruders – who had wire-tapping equipment, cameras, film, and several thousand dollars in cash in their possession. The burglars were taken to the police station and processed.

## ONE SIMPLE THING

*It was later discovered that the burglars had actually broken into the same offices three weeks earlier, but their mission had been unsuccessful. They had returned to fix wiretaps that were not working, and photograph additional confidential documents. The five men arrested were Bernard Barker, Virgillio Gonzalez, Eugenio Martinez, James McCord, and Frank Sturgis. They were charged with breaking into the headquarters of the Democratic National Committee at the Watergate Complex.*

*Later that year Frank Wills received a special award from the Democratic National Committee for playing "a unique role in the history of the nation."*

*As far as Frank was concerned, he was simply doing his job.*

# Chapter 8. One Simple Thing for 100 Days

> *If I can access a set of simple tools to see and understand my patterns and how they are helping or harming me, understand who I am, what is important, and how I want to connect with others in the world, and create a basic framework to guide my patterns of thought, behavior, and decision-making,* **then** *I can identify and accomplish One Simple Thing every day to reach my goal and realize a productive, sustainable, and fit life.*

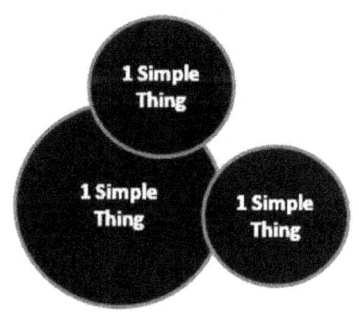

This is the hypothesis that began this work, and the pathway that will get you from where you are now, to where you want to be. To talk about a new way of thinking and being is to invite you into a space of inquiry and help you recognize that you do have the power to create the life you want and to influence the world around you. You started with a goal and a hypothesis, and you are ready to implement your own personal strategies and tactics, and live your own Theory of Change.

Each and every day there are opportunities to choose a path, to discover, to take a risk, and to boldly act. To support you on your journey toward fitness, this is an opportunity to explore and test-drive One Simple

Thing every day. Start with your own list of simple actions that you identified in the last chapter. From there you can continue to build upon your experiences and learning, as one thing can and often does lead to another.

In case you get stuck, the rest of this chapter offers you *One Simple Thing for 100 Days* to help you gather and maintain your momentum. They are broad enough to be universally applicable and open to your own interpretation. They are also precise enough to fit into the moment and your own particular circumstances. Don't be surprised if patterns emerge.

Note and track your successes and disappointments (yes, there will be disappointments, too!), what is changing, and what you are learning. Take heart and carry on in your efforts. This is more than a checklist or To-Do list. It is encouragement, confirmation, aspiration, possibility, and a different way of being in the world. See what you can see, and do, and change.

**Remember to act with intention. What do YOU want to have accomplished in the end?**

## ONE SIMPLE THING FOR 100 DAYS

1. Striving is about purpose. What one accomplishment can you point to today with pride?

2. Each of us is who we are. Take the time to demonstrate your authenticity with others today.

3. How fortunate that you have great people in your life who will stand beside you just because of who you are. Tell someone how much you appreciate them being there for you.

## Chapter 8. One Simple Thing for 100 Days

4. As your schedule for today unfolds, reflect and then choose where to best focus your time and energy.

5. It is who you are when no one is looking that counts. What action can you take today that will shout out who you really are to those around you?

6. Remember that every act has the potential to influence the future. How will you go about creating a meaningful ripple today?

7. Ask someone how they think you are doing. Be open to the feedback of others today, yet let your own judgment and values guide you.

8. Courage is yours every day you make a difficult decision. Today take one brave step outside of your comfort zone.

9. Make up your own mind. Ask one question today that helps you clarify your thinking about something important to you, and then act.

10. Do more than what is expected of you today and watch what happens. How does it feel?

11. Today let curiosity be your guide. Stand in a different space of inquiry, look around, and see what you can learn from another viewpoint.

12. Get into the habit of saying to others, "What can I do for you?" and mean it. Try it with someone you'd like to get to know better.

13. What you do will always speak louder than anything you say. What are your behaviors telling those around you right now? Is that your true message?

14. Whose voice do you listen to? Today start with your own voice, and then seek out new and diverse perspectives from others around you. What have you learned?

15. When faced with a critical decision today, your values and purpose will point the way. What path speaks loudest to you right now?

16. There is always the default option. Today, choose an unfamiliar and untested alternative and see where it leads you.

17. Knowing what you don't want is at least as important as knowing what you do want. How can you use this information to influence one decision today?

18. What if you did? What if you didn't? What will you choose to do differently today?

19. Trust yourself to handle today's challenges. Identify one resource you have not considered tapping into before, and see where it leads you.

20. Today take a giant step out of your comfort zone and pursue what creates meaning in your life. What can you discover?

21. Explore an issue you are not familiar with and then be there to support another's priorities.

22. You have complete control of your viewfinder. Today take the time to refocus on something you may have overlooked.

23. Identify one obstacle you have bumped into from time to time. What will you do today to make it over that hurdle?

## Chapter 8. One Simple Thing for 100 Days

24. Today, take the time to broaden your own perspective. Ask someone else for a reality check and go from there.

25. There is a difference between what you see and what you are looking for. How can you better explore your options today?

26. What do you need to do today to make a more informed decision? Identify a priority and get started.

27. Take time today to recognize the opportunities in front of you. Go out of your way to investigate a new angle and learn more about the possibilities that lie there.

28. Results often require a marathon and not a sprint. Think about one thing you've been putting off and get moving on it today.

29. Share an important idea with others, and light a spark in someone else to do what they have always wanted to do.

30. Doing what is right also means what is right for you. Today remind yourself what is important to you and stand firm when it comes time to make a choice.

31. Active listening is about being there for someone else. Share this gift with someone new today.

32. Successful relationships are tough to maintain, but don't have to be complicated. Start a conversation today and be yourself.

33. Engagement comes from the inside out; what one thing will ignite your passion today?

34. Today reach out and teach someone something they didn't even know they wanted to learn.

35. Everyone is connected to everyone else and someone close to you needs your help. How will you be there for them today when it counts?

36. Feedback helps keep you on course. If you don't know how you're doing, ask.

37. When was the last time you stopped and really thought about your needs? Today find some time to focus on you and your own priorities.

38. What Aha's are you seeing today, and which are you missing? Open your eyes and look again.

39. Today be sure to give your complete attention to someone else and listen to their story. What can you learn by asking one or two important questions?

40. Think about your power to make a difference. Watch the ripple effect that flows from one simple decision you make today.

41. Getting in touch with a different aspect of yourself can help you change the world. What will you discover about yourself today that you have not seen before?

42. A sense of urgency can be the impetus you need today. Shift your pace and see what happens.

43. Have a question? Look for the answer inside yourself first. You are your best resource.

## Chapter 8. One Simple Thing for 100 Days

44. Let go of one thing today that is holding you back. That is your first step forward.

45. Today offer to help someone who seems lost. You will both be rewarded by your generosity.

46. It is often the simple things that give you a true sense of accomplishment. Today, if it takes less than five minutes to do, do it now – and then happily cross it off your To-Do list.

47. Talent is meant to be shared. What can you give today that will be appreciated by others?

48. Next time someone needs to talk, really listen – with full attention, patience, and without judgment.

49. Laughter is an asset to be used generously. Today spread it around and watch what happens.

50. In a world that never stops moving, be prepared, and pay special attention today. Right now, what do you see?

51. Are you taking yourself too seriously? Today be sure to find the time for a good laugh at yourself.

52. Your energy and enthusiasm are contagious to everyone around you. What one thing can you do to share and generate that same feeling in others?

53. Try one new thing today. Take what you learn and then try another new thing tomorrow.

54. The freedom to make your own decisions comes with responsibility. Explore the implications of a decision you will make today on those around you.

55. Triumph is not about the absence of difficulty; it is about seeing, understanding, and then acting when faced with adversity. Remember that today when the going gets tough.

56. Yes, today is a busy day. Still, be sure to leave some time to relax and appreciate what you have.

57. Today invest in yourself. You are the product of all that you do, believe, and care about. What's your next move?

58. Next time you insist on having your own way, think about how it will affect those around you with less power or authority. Now what will you do?

59. Everyone needs their own space. Today, step back and allow someone to choose what they need for themselves. Now, how can you support them?

60. Things come and go; the people in our lives are what truly matter. In the heat of the moment today, remember what's really important.

61. What do you care about most? You carry that touchstone with you every day. Listen to what it is saying to you right now and act upon it.

62. Today contribute to a cause or an effort that will make a profound difference for you and others in your community.

## Chapter 8. One Simple Thing for 100 Days

63. Are you using all your gifts and talents? Take stock today and begin to access and use those that have been dormant.

64. Where would you like to be in three years? Five years? Ten years? What one step can you take today to help get you there?

65. Imagine what you could accomplish if you thought more broadly and more boldly. Today take the time to see and understand what you are truly capable of.

66. What do you want more (or less) of? Now that you have that figured out, what are you going to do about it today?

67. What theme consistently runs through your life? Pay attention: this is a pattern that is important to you! Is it time to **amp** or **damp?**

68. Hold close a clear image of your vision for yourself; that is your map and compass and transport. How will you maintain your focus today?

69. Everyone make mistakes – including you. Take a moment today for forgiveness, and let both yourself and others off the hook.

70. A smile, a nod, a handshake or a simple question can start a meaningful relationship for you today. Go for it.

71. Consistency and credibility go hand-in-hand; align your voice, your promises, and your actions in a troublesome situation today.

72. Simply be yourself today – the one and only – and think about what you can accomplish in one day just by being you.

73. We are better when we collaborate. How can you connect with and support another individual today?

74. When you inflame a situation, recognize it, understand it, and own it. What can you do differently next time?

75. Today, take a moment to breathe and give others a chance to catch up. Not everyone learns or thinks the same way you do.

76. Look around you; recognize and appreciate who is there right now for you.

77. Take a risk today and watch what happens. What risk will you take tomorrow?

78. Demonstrate respect and appreciation in word and deed today. It could be as simple as saying, "Thank you."

79. Do not allow yourself to be ruled by circumstances; accept that setback and move forward with grace.

80. Learning is a never-ending process; be on the lookout for new knowledge today and pass it on.

81. In your own unique way, approach your responsibilities today as opportunities to make a real difference. Recognize other champions around you, too.

82. Start where you are and use what you have. Now, where are you headed?

## Chapter 8. One Simple Thing for 100 Days

83. Believe you can – and you will! Cheerlead for yourself and your team today.

84. Letting go is not giving up: it is recognizing the illusion of control and appreciating your power of presence and influence. What is one way you will influence others today?

85. Today, if you have the chance to connect with someone or stand up for someone, just do it!

86. Some battles are worth fighting, some are not, and some are better left alone. Today, think about which are which, and why; and then act upon that insight.

87. Stick-to-itiveness is just that: recognize what needs to be done today, remember why, and then see it through.

88. No one can do it all by themselves. Today ask for help and support from those around you.

89. What is meaningful to you may be meaningful to others as well. Share your enthusiasm, open sense of wonder, and discovery.

90. Similarities and differences abound; your own and the gifts of others can seed many gardens today. How will you purposefully engage with others?

91. Today reach out with your voice and ideas. Be sure to keep your own mind and ears open to the voices of others, too.

92. What will your hard work today get you? Maybe nothing; maybe a giant step towards your dreams. What will you decide to do?

93. Keep an eye out today for others who share your passion and want to work beside you in fulfilling goals. Today might be the day to create a new, important team.

94. Take a step back to see and understand some old patterns around you. What one particular pattern do you see, and what are you going to do about it now?

95. Find the time today to identify and own your assumptions about what shapes the behaviors and choices of those around you. What have you discovered?

96. Make today about someone else; give them the opportunity to act upon their own ideas. What can you both learn and gain?

97. Today, show up and be sure you are giving the best that you've got. Be present in one way that is different for you.

98. Imagine if everyone around you were committed and encouraged to challenge the status quo. What can you do to inspire and support that effort?

99. Today you will have the choice to comply with or challenge a sticky situation in your life. Choose the most meaningful path for you.

100. Our stories are the essence of who we are. Today, be generous and share your story with someone new.

Chapter 8.  One Simple Thing for 100 Days

**Simple Things to Consider:**

- *When you wake up in the morning say to yourself aloud, "I will do One Simple Thing today to make a difference; and that is ..."*

# *GRACE*

*When talking about change I think it is important to recognize that learning and growth are not always planned, nor is the path always straight. My own long and winding road, for example, represents an unceasing, persistent process that encompasses my personal, professional, and spiritual development. I have enthusiastically anticipated the unknown, and embraced change when it has presented itself.*

*I feel confident and sure in saying that my life really is about change, and can even point to specific instances. I also believe that the extent of my transformation will be measured by the deliberate and evolving vision and application of my new learning and shifting patterns.*

*Each new idea I have and sentence I write is a vision and application of new learning and shifting patterns; every added connection and interpretation of incoming data is a vision and application of new learning and shifting patterns; each observation, explanation, and analysis of people, places, and phenomena around me is a vision and application of new learning and shifting patterns; every new sentence and reference in my life's ongoing*

## ONE SIMPLE THING

*narrative is a vision and application of new learning and shifting patterns; every dialogue and discussion I have with myself, colleagues and friends, fellow travelers, and explorers at home or on the road is a vision and application of new learning and shifting patterns; and each and every relationship, interaction, communication, and exchange I have had with the world at large is a demonstration of integration, consumption, reflection, expanding vision, and intentional application of new learning and shifting patterns.*

*The fusing of these actions, in concert with my ability to better and more broadly be, think, discuss, write, connect, teach, touch, understand, and change my world, is the true measure of my capacity: to learn and grow and be my best self.*

*Here I am.*

# Chapter 9. The Individual, the Whole, and the Greater Whole

We are constantly growing, changing, and seeking a fit between ourselves and our world. Because of this, there is a never-ending flutter of movement – not from point A to point B, but rather a rash of constantly erupting skirmishes in response to the world. We imagine cycling through one set of experiences and moving on, thinking we are going to get "there" someday. Perhaps a more productive and healthier strategy is to acknowledge where we are now, realize where we want to go, and decide how we are going to get there moment by moment, action by action.

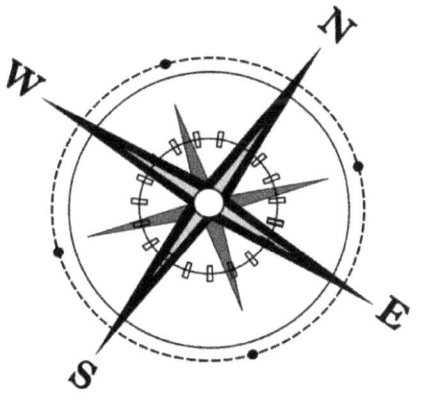

The horizon we aim for is a life that is coherent and consistent with our values and beliefs. With each step forward, our vistas shift and our prospects appear broader and more defined. Just as we must feel safe and secure and in sync within our environment, we can recognize and appreciate that we are not simply working toward a singular result. Instead we are reaching out for the right wavelength that can be understood and embraced. This is not a solitary purpose but a composite of the ends and means. As the landscape moves, what we hold on to is finding the right fit for us.

## ONE SIMPLE THING

People tend to get what they look for, whether it is scarcity or abundance. If I believe that I will never get the resources to meet my wants and needs, then that will be the truth. You, too, may believe that true opportunities are few and far between. On the other hand, believing in and living with a frame of reference firmly fixed in a space of abundance, you know there are always plenty of new chances, choices, and opportunities.

As I meet and accomplish the goals I have set, I can celebrate and learn from each step forward. I can appreciate there are specific things I can do along the way, that help me understand the patterns in my life – those which have enabled and supported me, and those which have deterred and defeated me. And if I can be my own best self, I can choose from the broad array of options in front of me. I can influence my life, and impact the world.

In case you haven't noticed, this is a highly "you-centered" approach, designed to meet your specific needs and learning, growth and achievement. Living your own Theory of Change is an opportunity to challenge and trust yourself, examine your own thinking and performance, and stand in your own space of inquiry.

This process motivates you to be your absolute best, to achieve extraordinary results, to be consciously competent, and to find your own joy. Why? Because it is about YOU: your results and your own achievement. Not only have you created an honest partnership with yourself, but you are also engaging in very specific and personal tests. Identifying and examining your patterns allows for almost immediate, direct feedback, and this link between your behavior and outcomes is a means for seeking truth with your own talents and skills.

As you embark on this personal journey, seek out experiences that will help you practice and reinforce your new patterns. Identify and address obstacles in your path, adding those new competencies to your wealth of assets. Continue to develop your new learning, seeking and accepting

## Chapter 9. The Individual, the Whole, and the Greater Whole

support along the way from those around you, those who care about you and your success.

Travel on and you will reach a clearer understanding of your strengths and vulnerabilities, gain an aptitude and knack for influencing, and expand yourself with each action and interaction. All the while, you will be developing further insights and awareness about complexity, human systems dynamics, and those around you. This supports establishing and maintaining strong relationships and setting a bright course for tomorrow.

As for the future, continue to stand in that space of inquiry and pay attention to your patterns and self-dialogues. Test and revisit your Personal Inventory, DecisionScapes, and Simple Rules to check that they are still the right ones for you. Each day seek out and accomplish at least One Simple Thing, and maintain that sweet spot in your viewfinder. Naturally, there will always be questions:

- What do I want to be working on?
- What do I need to help others realize and discover?
- What do I want to change?
- What do I want to create?

*You will figure it out.*

Do not forget that we are all connected; *WE* are all *US*. It is not always easy to see the quicksilver thread that links us to other persons, places, things, and events. That is especially true when more and more often we seem to communicate through talking points, texts, and selfies. Nothing stands alone, there is no one and only solution to a problem, and large and small actions both create amazing ripples in endless streams. Everything you do is about the individual, the whole, and the greater whole.

*Be wise and always act with intention.*

## ONE SIMPLE THING

We are at a crossroad in our lives beyond age, time, place, race, politics, or economics. Each of us can envision and support universal public goods. And each of us can make a conscious and meaningful choice between abundance and scarcity, resilience and despair, change and …. ?

Take this time and opportunity to magnify and examine the patterns and significance of your behaviors. The secret to knowing yourself lies in your own questions.

Embrace the notion that *One Simple Thing can and will change everything, that YOU can change everything.*

**And just imagine: what if everyone did that?!**

 **One Last Simple Thing to Consider:**

Last year I was flying home from Minneapolis and received a text notification that I had been awarded an upgrade to first class. No, I am not a road warrior, and frankly air travel is no longer quite the glamorous experience I remember it being when I was a kid. This, however, was a pleasant treat. The flight was less than three hours, so there was no meal and I do not drink; still the advantages of a comfy seat, extra leg room, and getting on and off the airplane sooner rather than later, were obvious. Here I was settled in 2C, with all the cranberry juice and salty snacks I wanted.

Chapter 9. The Individual, the Whole, and the Greater Whole

Almost all the passengers had boarded when several crew members carried on a severely disabled young man and took him to his seat in the rear of the cabin. He was someone's son; he could have been my son.

This was definitely a no-brainer. I stopped an attendant and told her I wanted to give up my seat for the young man. We swapped and soon were on our way. I can still see the look on his face. He could not thank me enough nor believe *his good fortune*. The young man graciously bought me a drink – so I did get my full supply of cranberry juice – and an attendant gave me a bunch of first class snacks to munch on throughout the flight.

Even at my most cynical, this is the way I look at it: I did not earn my upgrade and I did not pay for the space in first class. By the luck of the draw my name was the next one on the upgrade list; and I could walk on and off this airplane all by myself. It was an easy decision. What surprised me was the number of folks who came up to me and told me what a wonderful thing I'd done. *Really?* Well, perhaps this One Simple Thing will create a ripple, too, and influence someone else some other time.

It's amazing that One Simple Thing can remind us of how much we have to be grateful for, how simple it is to share and multiply what we have with others, and how simple it is to make a difference in the life of another. I won't forget the smile on that young man's face. That, too, was One Simple Thing.

# THE SIMPLE RULES FOUNDATION

## You Can Be One In A Million

**Our Mission** is to empower you to create your own simple rules to shift your patterns to a productive, sustainable life. We facilitate, educate, train, coach, guide, and support YOU – individuals, families, organizations and communities – in creating and amplifying sustainability and productivity around the world. We invite you to join us today in this undertaking.

- Visit us at **www.simplerulesfoundation.org** to find out more about our work.
- Send us your simple rules and share your ideas.
- Contribute to creating a better life for yourself and others.
- **Be One In a Million and change the world!**

SIMPLE RULES FOUNDATION
Be One in a Million and Change the World.

# Reference and Resources

Anderson, A. (2005). *The Community Builder's Approach to Theory of Change.* Washington, DC: Aspen Institute.

Annie E. Casey Foundation. (2004). *Theory of Change: A Practical Tool for Action, Results, and Learning.* Seattle, WA: Organizational Research Services.

Auspos, P. & Cabaj, M. (2014). *Complexity and Community Change: Managing Effectively to Improve Effectiveness.* Washington, DC: Aspen Institute.

Borah, A. (2014) *India's Rain Forest Man.* Retrieved from http://www.aljazeera.com/indepth/features/2014/01/indias-forest-man-201411762848958203.html.

Bridges, W. (2009). *Managing Transitions: Making the Most of Change.* Boston, MA: Da Capo Press.

Dozois, E., Langolis, M., Blanchet-Cohen, N. (2010). *A Practitioner's Guide to Developmental Evaluation.* Vancouver, BC: International Institute for Child Rights and Development.

Eoyang, G. (1997). *Coping with Chaos: Seven Simple Tools.* Circle Pines, MN: Lagumo.

Eoyang, G. & Holladay, R. (2013). *Adaptive Action: Leveraging Uncertainty in Your Organization.* Stanford, CA: Stanford University Press.

Flynn, M., Treasure-Evans, J., & Green, D. (2012). *Theory of Change: What's It All About?* Retrieved from http://www.intrac.org/data/files/resources/741/ONTRAC-51-Theory-of-Change.pdf.

Forti, M. (2012). *Six Theory of Change Pitfalls to Avoid.* Stanford Social Innovation Review. May 23, 2012. Retrieved from http://www.ssireview.org/blog/entry/six_theory_of_change_pitfalls_to_avoid.

Hart, E. W. & Kirkland, K. (2001) *Using Your Executive Coach.* Greensboro, NC: Center for Creative Leadership.

Holladay, R. (2005) *Simple Rules: Organizational DNA.* OD Practitioner 37 (4).

Mackinnon, A., Amott, N. & McGarvey, C. (2010). *Mapping Change: Using a Theory of Change to Guide Planning and Evaluation.* New York, NY: The Foundation Center.

Nevid, J. S. (2014) *Essentials of Psychology: Concepts and Applications.* Boston, MA: Cengage Learning.

O'Connor. J & McDermott, I. (1997). *The Art of Systems thinking: Essential Skills for Creativity and Problem Solving.* London, UK: Thorsons.

OECD (2012), *Evaluating Peacebuilding Activities in Settings of Conflict and Fragility: Improving Learning for Results.* DAC Reference Series, OECD Publishing. Retrieved at http://dx.doi.org/10.1787/9789264106802-en.

Research and Training Center for Children's Mental Health. (2009). *Understanding Theories of Change: A Theory-Based Approach to Change, Complexity, and Accountability*. Tampa, FL University of South Florida.

Stacey, R. D. (1995). *The Science of Complexity: An Alternative Perspective for Strategic Change Processes.* Strategic Management Journal, Vol. 16, No. 6.

Sweeney, L. B. (2008). *Connected Wisdom: Living Stories about Living Systems.* Hong Kong: Regent Publishing Services Ltd.

Taplin, D. H., & Clark, H. (2012). *Theory of Change Basics: A Primer on Theory of Change.* New York, NY: Center for Human Environments.

Ting, S. & Scisco, P. (Eds.) (2006). *The CCL Handbook of Coaching: A Guide for the Leader Coach.* San Francisco, CA: Jossey-Bass.

Tytel, M. (2009*). Vision Driven: Lessons Learned from the Small Business C-Suite.* Apache Junction, AZ: Gold Canyon Press.

Tytel, M. & Holladay, R. (2011) *Radical Inquiry Journal: A Companion Tool for Simple Rule*s. Apache Junction, AZ: Gold Canyon Press.

Tytel, M. & Holladay, R. (2011). *Simple Rules: A Radical Inquiry into Self.* Apache Junction, AZ: Gold Canyon Press.

## SIR ALEXANDER FLEMING

http://www.acs.org/content/acs/en/education/whatischemistry/landmarks/flemingpenicillin.html

http://digital.nls.uk/scientists/biographies/alexander-fleming/

http://www.chemheritage.org/discover/online-resources/chemistry-in-history/themes/pharmaceuticals/preventing-and-treating-infectious-diseases/fleming.aspxResources

http://www.britannica.com/EBchecked/topic/209952/Sir-Alexander-Fleming

## ROSA PARKS

http://www.archives.gov/education/lessons/rosa-parks/

https://www.thehenryford.org/exhibits/rosaparks/story.asp

http://www.achievement.org/autodoc/page/par0int-1

http://www.biography.com/people/rosa-parks-9433715#synopsis

## FRANK WILLS

http://www.senate.gov/artandhistory/history/common/investigations/Watergate.htm

## References and Resources

http://www.fordlibrarymuseum.gov/museum/exhibits/watergate_files/

http://americanhistory.about.com/od/watergate/f/watergate.htm

http://www.theguardian.com/news/2000/oct/10/guardianobituaries.haroldjackson

## SELECTED WEBSITES

ActKnowledge:
www.actknowledge.org

Appalachian Trail Conservancy:
www.appalachiantrail.org

BOIDS:
http://www.red3d.com/cwr/boids/

Healthy Workplaces:
www.healthyworkplaces.com
www.vision-driven.net

Human Systems Dynamics Institute:
www.hsdinstitute.org
http://wiki.hsdinstitute.org

The Aspen Institute:
www.aspeninstitute.org

The Center for Theory of Change:
www.theoryofchange.org

Third Sector New England:
www.TSNE.org

The Simple Rules Foundation:
www.simplerulesfoundation.org
www.simplerules.org

# About the Author

Dr. Mallary Tytel is president and founder of *Healthy Workplaces*, a national consulting practice. Her work focuses on complexity science and human systems dynamics, facilitation and coaching, diversity and culture, developing women leaders, and building productive and sustainable workplaces.

She is the former CEO of an international nonprofit human resource development corporation; has served as a key advisor to senior-level civilian and military personnel in the U.S. Department of Defense; and created and delivered an innovative leadership training program in over 40 diverse communities worldwide. Most recently Mallary co-founded *The Simple Rules Foundation*, whose mission is to help individuals, organizations and communities see, understand, and influence the patterns around them.

Mallary has a PhD in Public Health Promotion and Organizational Systems from the Union Institute and University, an MBA from the University of Connecticut, and is a certified mediator and certified executive coach. In her spare time she writes and mentors budding women entrepreneurs.

Dr. Tytel may be reached at
mallary@simplerulesfoundation.org

www.ingramcontent.com/pod-product-compliance
Lightning Source LLC
Chambersburg PA
CBHW071422160426
43195CB00013B/1772